# THE
# PURE
# LOVER

# THE
# PURE
# LOVER

*A Memoir of Grief*

DAVID PLANTE

BEACON PRESS | BOSTON

Beacon Press
25 Beacon Street
Boston, Massachusetts 02108-2892
www.beacon.org

Beacon Press books
are published under the auspices of
the Unitarian Universalist Association of Congregations.

12  11  10  09    8  7  6  5  4  3  2  1

This book is printed on acid-free paper that meets the uncoated paper
ANSI/NISO specifications for permanence as revised in 1992.

Text design and composition by Susan E. Kelly
at Wilsted & Taylor Publishing Services

Most information about the history of the Italian invasion and German occupation
of Greece, and of the Civil War, comes from *Red Acropolis, Black Terror,* by Andre
Gerolymatos, and information about Benaki Hall from *Memoirs of a Witness:
The German Occupation of Athens College (1941–1944),* by George S. Phylactopoulos.

The photograph that is the frontispiece was taken in 1966, in Sloane Square, London,
by the Greek writer Costas Tachsis. (Photograph courtesy of Costas Tachsis.)

Library of Congress Cataloging-in-Publication Data
Plante, David.
  The pure lover : a memoir of grief / David Plante.
     p. cm.
  ISBN 978-0-8070-7298-1 (alk. paper)
  1. Plante, David—Relations with men.  2. Stangos, Nikos.
3. Novelists, American—20th century—Biography.  I. Title.
  PS3566.L257Z47 2009
  305.4′092′2—dc22
  [B]                                        2009010399

In a notebook I found of yours, you wrote a poem called

*The Pure Lover*

which you crossed out.

The last line, crossed out, is:

*Please let me make the fragments meaningful.*

# Also by David Plante

# THE
# PURE
# LOVER

# PROLOGUE

Nikos Stangos died April 16, 2004. We had been loving partners for some forty years. He died of cancer—of the lungs, spine, and brain. I was with him when he died, in our bed, after six months of physical and mental deterioration. All the while, I kept a daily diary, but only after his death did I find myself compelled to write down separately—now no longer a part of daily life but within the sphere of grief—the thoughts and feelings that came to me. Recollections came to me at home, out on a walk, suddenly in a market, waiting in an airport terminal, one after the other, without any order that I was aware of. It was as if all my nearly forty years of life with Nikos contracted into no time, into no place, as if from outside our day-to-day relationship, so a recollection from late in our lives together was followed by one from the very beginning, an event remembered from his last weeks in London followed by one long before, in Greece or Italy. No doubt some inner reckoning of my grief was evolving. These notes seemed to me spontaneous but random, yet I sensed that grief knew more than I did about the evolution of grief, knew something whole while I knew only flashes of the whole.

Perhaps it is a stage in grief's evolution to want to try to put some order in the notes I took, much in the same way there is a stage in grief when the bereaved suddenly wants to put order in his lost lover's clothes, papers, the effects in his desk drawers. Over and over, I arranged and rearranged the notes—the markings of grief's way—and slowly tried for some coherence in time and place.

Do the fragments come together as a whole? I imagine this: an invisible Greek amphora, larger than all the assembled fragments, shaping the larger invisible whole.

# Alpha

*Grief has grief's own will.*

In 1921, inspired by the Great Idea—Μεγάλι Ιδέα—of reclaiming the Byzantine Empire from the Turks and the Bulgarians, Greece went to war with those two countries, and lost. Accused, six ministers, the former prime minister among them, were lined up in a field outside Athens and shot.

After the defeat of Greece in Turkey and Bulgaria, the Greek, Turkish, and Bulgarian governments agreed to a treaty that stipulated the exchange of populations. Greece expelled Turkish-speaking Muslims to Turkey, and Turkey expelled Orthodox Greeks to Greece. Bulgaria expelled the Greek population. After 1923, refugees from Turkey and Bulgaria formed a fifth of the population of Greece. This was known as the Catastrophe—Καταστροφή.

You told me your father was from an ancient Greek town, originally called Apollonia then changed to Sosopol, Bulgaria, on the Black Sea. Your grandfather owned a fleet of ships and had the biggest house in the town. He sent his sons to be educated abroad, in Berlin and Paris, and your father to MIT in Cambridge, Massachusetts, where he studied engineering and architecture. Your father never returned to Bulgaria, but his father refused to leave Sosopol, where he had never learned Bulgarian and was known for having shot to death a Bulgarian for looking at one of his daughters. Refusing to leave, you said, he climbed a tree and never came down, which meant he hanged himself. His family was dispersed, some in Salonika, some in Athens, including your father.

You told me your mother was from Constantinople, from an old Greek family who, you believed, had lived there since Byzantine times. She had never been to Greece, which she considered to be Albania, Athens a dusty, provincial town. When forced to leave, her family saved some Turkish rugs and silver. They moved to Athens.

Your mother and father had met as students at Robert's College, in Constantinople, and while your father had been in America, they had courted each other with letters written in English. In Athens, where they married, your parents were part of the mass of refugees disdained by the natives, most of them living in camps, in packed churches, in back alleys. Educated, upper middle class, your parents had enough gold sovereigns from your mother's dowry to sustain them.

Your father managed to get work designing and overseeing the new Athens College, Benaki Hall, in the suburb of Athens called Psychiko, where he and your mother lived, and where you spent your first years.

You were born, November 1936, into a dictatorship, that of Ioannis Metaxas, a deputy minister who, with the support of King George II, had in August 1936 suspended articles of the constitution and imposed martial law to stop a general strike of the Workers' Federation, the strike caused by the destitution wrought by the worldwide Depression. Metaxas saw the strike as a Communist threat and its perpetrators as traitors and anti-Christian. Thousands of suspects were arrested, many tortured and condemned to prison. In reaction, the Communist Party grew.

You were an unwanted child, conceived accidentally. Your father wanted your mother to have an abortion, which she refused to have. It was on the day of your birth that the bones of King Constantine, father of King George II, who had died in exile in Palermo, Sicily, ten years before, were returned to Greece. You were born in a clinic, where your mother arrived just in time because of the procession and parades and crowds for the return of the exiled king's bones. You were born on November 21, but your father registered your birth a day late, on November 22.

It was an age of dictatorships. The Italian dictator Benito Mussolini threatened the Greek dictator Metaxas with invasion on October 28, 1940. Metaxas bluntly refused to accept Mussolini's demands, saying "*Oxi!*" ("No!"), and the Italians invaded. The Greek army repulsed the Italians into Albania.

Though the fascist Italians failed to invade and occupy Greece, the Nazi Germans succeeded. As there was no penicillin, the dictator Metaxa died of tonsillitis. The prime minister who succeeded him committed suicide. The king and what was left of the government sought refuge in Cairo, Egypt, but the Egyptian government refused to allow the Greek king to stay. The British offered him refuge in London.

The last rearguard action by the Greek army against the Germans was at Thermopylae.

On April 27, 1941, the Germans entered Athens through empty streets.

You were four and a half years old.

In the Psychiko suburb of Athens, the large neoclassical building of Athens College, Benaki Hall, which your father had designed and where the elite of Greek young men were taught, was taken over by the Germans and made into a hospital for their own use.

Street names were changed from Greek into German or Italian.

The Germans commandeered all produce, and famine spread among the people. In Athens alone, more than one hundred thousand died of starvation.

Each morning, trucks collected corpses to take them to the outskirts of Athens, where they were unloaded into pits. When lack of fuel almost stopped this collection, decaying bodies were piled on street corners. Skeletal children watched over dead parents.

Your family were living now outside Athens, between the airport and the sea, in Elleniko: your parents, your grandmother on your mother's side, a maid, a cook, and a gardener. Your father worked in Athens, in his own office, as architect and civil engineer. Your mother did gardening along with the gardener, and, as you grew, you did also. You liked to watch the water course through the narrow channels the gardener dug to water the trees, each channel with a little dam that you broke through to let the water flow through the channel. You remembered learning the Latin alphabet before the Greek, singing *abcdefg*

*hijk*

*lmnop*

while fitting the cutout letters into a plywood board your father had brought back from America.

The female cat, for which you as hardly more than a baby had no strong feelings, gave birth to a litter. The gardener drowned the kittens in a bucket of water, you helping to poke them under the water with a stick. The guilt you felt later lasted all your life, and made you love cats as if to make up for your cruelty.

You had no relationships with anyone except with the cat whose litter you had helped kill, the maid, Loxandra, your grandmother, and your mother, in that order. You had no friends, and hardly went outside the garden. You loved music. You were obstinate and difficult and not very cheerful. You loved eating, wandering in the garden, and watching the washerwomen, the large bodies in loose, wet clothes, in the laundry shed, washing the sheets in the rising steam. You loved hiding in the unused garage and the dark potting shed where the gardener kept his tools and insect repellent for the pistachio trees, the lemon, tangerine, almond, Seville orange trees, the gigantic clippers for cutting the caterpillar cocoons from the pine trees, the big clear glass globes that were hung on the branches with blossoms of the female pistachio trees after they had been hung on the branches of the male trees to collect the pollen. Vegetables, onions, artichokes, wheat were grown in the garden. There was a mimosa tree that seemed always to be in blossom, the scent of which rose to the bedroom windows, and there was a huge bougainvillea over the main entrance.

Many of the German collaborators belonged to ethnic minorities, such as Turkish-speaking Christians; some consisted of Greek-speaking villagers sympathetic to the rightist National Republican Greek League (EDES) fleeing from Communist persecution by the leftist Greek People's Liberation Army (ELAS); and many others consisted of criminals attracted by plunder. Some were employed by the Germans to discourage resistance by terrorism: they were described as "death squads." The members committed such atrocities that the Germans hanged twelve of them.

Loxandra was a Communist. She was devoted to you and your mother, but tyrannized everyone else in the family, even your father. Often, your grandmother locked herself in her bedroom because she was frightened of Loxandra.

Your father developed a throat infection, which no amount of lemon juice would alleviate. The infection worsened and began to affect his lungs. He wore his pajamas and dressing gown all day, and it seemed to you that when, walking unsteadily across a room, your father bumped into the edge of a table or the back of a chair, the cloth of the dressing gown would give way as if your father did not have a body beneath.

Your grandmother died during the hot summer. Her body was laid out on her bed, the door closed. From time to time, you went into the room, alone, to see your dead grandmother, and, too, to touch her face, which was cold and hard. You were fascinated that she was dead. She seemed to be sweating a little.

The death penalty was imposed for listening to Allied radio broadcasts, distributing Allied propaganda leaflets, and hoarding food.

A German officer in the air force was billeted in your house. He was called Herr Werner. Loxandra told you to stay away from him.

Your father spent most of the day in the sitting room, which had a view of the garden through French windows; on a round table next to him was the radio, shortwave, which you remembered him switching off if he heard the officer enter the house. But if Herr Werner came in without being heard, he would stop at the doorway and ask if he could listen with your father to the BBC World Service, announced with the strokes of Big Ben. You sometimes listened with your father and Werner. As you all listened, Loxandra would bring in cups of mock-coffee, made from the roasted beans of a carob tree in the garden, along with glasses of cold water on a tray covered with an embroidered cloth.

There was no sugar for making *gliko*, jam. Your mother would not accept any from Werner, as she told you later, not only because she knew that the Germans had requisitioned all food for themselves, including olive oil, which was sent to Germany to be made into margarine, but because acceptance would have outraged Loxandra.

In far Macedonia, a school was used as an interrogation center by the German supported right wing, EDES, the walls smeared with blood where the torturers wiped their hands.

While your father was napping in his room upstairs, you sat in your father's armchair by the window and looked out at the garden. The gardener was hoeing around a line of pumpkins, the seeds for which his father had brought back from America. Your father liked pumpkin pie.

Alone in the sitting room, but as if you were being watched, you reached out slowly to switch on the radio, and, sitting back in the chair, you listened to Bach partitas, which you had already heard enough times to be familiar with them.

You wanted to be a pianist, but you knew your parents would not allow you to. Your parents wanted you to be a doctor.

In a village, ELAS, which became the military arm of the Communist Party, arrested fourteen men. Their punishments were to set an example for all the local inhabitants, witnesses, in the village square, of the men, each in turn, stripped then tied to a table, arms spread open, for the blood-splattered murderer to hack at the screaming man's body with an axe—slowly, to prolong the agony.

The butchery was so prolonged for one man that a British officer present shot the man with his revolver to end his agony.

You did not leave the walled-in garden, where you wandered day after day as the summer gave way to autumn. You always found yourself at the east wall, the wall that separated your garden from the German soldiers' canteen. You leaned your head against the wall to listen to the record of a woman singing in German in a deep voice, a voice that at times sounded like a man's, a record that was played again and again. You heard laughter. You could not imagine what the German soldiers were doing behind the wall, in the midst of the singing.

Quietly, so no one would know, you sometimes went up to Werner's room, the door to which he always left open. Sunlight filled the room and doubled the furniture in the pale yellow marble of the floor. You noted, hung on the back of a chair, a military shirt, its sleeves rolled up. On the top of a chest of drawers, piled neatly, were clean underpants; undershirts; socks, military. Hanging about the knob of a drawer was a thin silver chain with a cross. You walked around to the other side of the beds where, on the floor, were underpants. There was a smell in the room of hair cream.

If your mother had to go out, you waited for her by the gate to the outside world. Sometimes you stood just outside the gate, on the dirt sidewalk. Outside the gate of the canteen next door was a German guard with a holstered pistol at his hip, wearing a helmet. One day, waiting for your mother, you saw that by the soldier was a stack of wooden crates. A small military truck drew up before the soldier and he shouted something to the driver, who got out and followed the guard into the canteen. In the back of the truck were, you saw, wicker baskets of potatoes. You also saw, across the street, at the edge of a thistle field, a boy. The boy's head was shaved, and he wore only shorts and a man's torn suit jacket, and as, suddenly, he ran across the street towards the truck, you saw that he was barefoot and that his legs were very thin, his knees large. The boy got to the truck, reached into a basket for a potato, and, just as he was running away with the large, black potato held to his chest, the German guard came out of the gate and shouted, "*Alt, alt,*" but the boy kept running. The guard took out his pistol, called "*Alt*" again, then shot, and the boy's shadow appeared to run on as he tripped and fell, then lay still, without a shadow, in the bright light. Loxandra pulled you inside.


You weren't asleep when the door to your room, always kept half open, opened completely, and you saw, against the light from the hall, your father come in followed by Werner, who was taller than your father. You shut your eyes but sensed the men standing above your head.

You heard Werner say about you, "He looks like an angel."

"Or a little devil," your father said, and laughed.


You got out of bed and went quietly downstairs.

Loxandra was at the kitchen table, reading, by the light of a stub candle, a pamphlet with pages so thin the light showed through them when she turned one. Her head was resting on one hand, and her black hair fell over her face. She drew her hair back and held it when she heard you come in.

"What do you want?" she asked.

"Nothing," you said.

She reached out for you and held you, her arms crossed over your chest, pressed against her.

One afternoon, wandering with your cat through the garden, you stopped at the east wall and leaned your head against it. There was silence from the canteen.

Your cat in your arms, you found Werner under the bougainvillea, as if waiting for you.

Werner said, in English, "You love your cat."

"I love her."

"You must keep her safe."

"Is there a danger?"

"People can become so hungry they will do terrible things."

The cat jumped out of your arms and ran into the garden.

Werner looked up into the bougainvillea, sighed, then looked back down at you.

He asked, "Would you like a ride in my airplane?"

Amazed, you simply nodded.

"Shall we go now?"

Again, you simply nodded.

"I'll go ask your father."

"No, don't," you said. "Don't."

"You're sure you don't want me to ask your father first?"

"Don't ask my father."

Werner laughed and said, "Then I won't ask him," and he put his hands on your shoulders.

You were given a ride in a *Stuka*.

You would not believe Loxandra when she told you what the German *Stuka* bombers did.

Seventy-eight prominent citizens of Lamia were executed by the Germans, one hundred and seventeen in Sparta, two hundred at Kaissariani, the entire male population of Kalavryta, of Distomo. The trucks carrying the dead dripped with blood, the graves were mass graves.

Werner did not return to his room one night. You slept and woke, slept and woke; sometimes, awake, you imagined you were seeing the open door to Werner's room in your sleep, and, asleep, you dreamed you saw Werner standing in the doorway to your room.

Outside, there were German voices, and the sound of boots on the gravel and on the marble stoop; the doorbell rang.

Your mother, putting on a dressing gown, rushed into your room and whispered, "Quickly, go to your father."

Loxandra was calling from downstairs.

You waited in a chair by your father, in bed, propped up by many pillows because he had a sore throat and couldn't swallow properly while lying down. You were both silent, and listened.

Your mother came into the bedroom and said, "Werner is dead. They insist we go to the funeral." She sat on the edge of the bed and put her hands to her forehead. "I told them you were too ill, but they insist I go. How can I go to the funeral of a German? I can't. I can't."

"What did Loxandra say?" your father asked.

"She said, 'We're all equal in death.' "

Your father smiled a little.

Your mother asked for the address of Werner's mother in Austria, and wrote a letter expressing her sorrow at the death of her son.

Your father remained in bed. His room was kept dim. Your mother sat for hours by your father. She asked you to sit by him each morning and afternoon, for an hour each time, even if it was to watch your father asleep. Your father's face was thin, his eyes closed; you did not know if he was asleep or not.

To amuse your father, your mother, for Halloween, dressed you as a girl and sent you into your father's room. Delirious, your father didn't recognize you, and shouted.
You ran out of the room, terrified.

You were sent into Athens to stay with your Aunt Tato.

You recalled, years later, hearing, in the mornings, men pulling wooden barrows along the streets below and calling, "Bring out your dead."

You recalled a suitcase filled with drachmas. You recalled useless drachma notes drifting about in puddles.

You did not want to live in Athens. You wanted your garden, where you wandered among the pistachio trees and orange and lemon trees, and where, looking for your cat, you went deeper among the trees until, turning back, you no longer saw the front of the house. Stalking insects, your cat came through the chamomile to you.

Your father died the day the Germans evacuated Athens, October 12, 1944. You were just short of eight years old.

The Germans, on withdrawing from the provinces, left collaborators garrisoned with supplies of weapons, and also left depots of arms within reach of ELAS, deliberately fomenting civil war.

The last German unit, which was stationed in Benaki Hall at Athens College, dumped all their extra ammunition in the air defense trenches of the campus and set fire to them before leaving, then went on to lower the Nazi flag from the Acropolis and lay a wreath on the Tomb of the Unknown Soldier, and they, too, left Athens.

Back in the house in Elleniko with your mother and Loxandra, you spent most of your time lying on your bed and watching the light on the ceiling.

Only two months after the German evacuation of Greece, civil war began between the forces of ELAS and the forces of EDES.

The British, who had supported ELAS during the German occupation but who now supported EDES, bombed the airport. As Elleniko was near the airport, it was in the range of the bombardments. You remembered crouching under the dining room table with Loxandra and your mother, both of whom sat on the floor, doubled over. A bomb fell near, and another, so near that a window broke in another room at the impact. Your body jolted. Loxandra was smiling, but her eyes were darkly circled and her face was stark. You laughed. As she often did, she put an arm around your shoulders and drew you to her. Then another bomb fell and the shock wave blasted through a dining room window. Loxandra held you more closely. Your laughter was high, shaking. Loxandra, after the sounds gave way to a strange silence, crawled out from beneath the table. You didn't move until she came back under the table on all fours and said it was all over. Your mother opened her eyes.


Aunt Tato insisted that your mother and you must come stay with her in Athens.

She said, "It is not possible to stay in Elleniko any longer, by the airport. The Germans were at least disciplined. But with the British around, there's no knowing what will happen."

"What about Loxandra?" your mother asked.

Aunt Tato raised her hands. "Loxandra? Loxandra can take care of herself."

"We can't get along without her."

"Very well. Very well. Very well."


You recalled seeing the acronym ΕΛΑΣ, a pun on the Greek word for Greece, ELAS, painted in red on walls.


Having to leave your cat behind in Elleniko, you would stand on the balcony of the apartment house and watch, in the distance outside Athens, flares lighting up the night in order for the British to bomb the airport, and you would worry about your cat, never again seen.

Loxandra lived in the maid's room, off the kitchen. She brought you to Communist rallies.

After preparing a meal of bean soup, Loxandra went into her room off the kitchen and came back wearing a steel helmet, with pistols at her hips, shoulder straps of cartridges, and a maiden-zone of hand grenades. Her work done for the family, she was going out to fight.

Alone in the kitchen, you lifted the lid on a pot of soup and, in a moment of strange perversity, threw a light bulb inside. Loxandra discovered this and told your aunt, whose accusations you denied. Your aunt said, "I saw you," and you, indignant that she should lie to you, retorted, "You couldn't have seen me, the door was shut."

Aunt Tato managed to get a live chicken. The problem in the family was: who would kill it? Loxandra grabbed the chicken by the neck and said, "Do you think I'm upset about killing a chicken? I kill men every night."

During battles, the family cowered in the small apartment at the top of the apartment house behind the Athens cathedral, and when the fighting stopped, you would go out onto the balcony to collect the shell casings.

Defeated in the Battle of Athens, ELAS continued to fight in the mountains.

You and your mother went to Elleniko to see what state the house was in. She had had a dream that the house was in danger from the British. In fact, it was occupied by British soldiers, who had torn up floorboards to light a fire in the fireplace. The furniture was in shambles. One British soldier was just then trying to sell what could be removed from the house to a Greek. You stood by your mother as she told the soldier that she was a poor widow, and, please, this was her home. The soldier stopped. But you and your mother never returned to live in your home.

Loxandra made you swear that you would work for the principles of the Communist Party for the rest of your life. She said to you, "Doesn't the outside world matter? Doesn't it? Well, if it does, then the Party does, because the Party is for the world, the whole outside world, everyone. The Party makes the whole world matter."

Loxandra waited, waited for the Communist army to return to Athens and, according to her, to liberate the city from the king, returned from London, and the monarchist government, but they did not come down from the mountains, the stark, snowbound mountains.

Loxandra killed herself by drinking toilet cleaner, made with sulfuric acid.

Benaki Hall was restored to Athens College. But on the very day the college reclaimed the hall, a Communist Kapetanios came and at gunpoint took away everything except doors, windows, radiators, all in the name of the people.

You started your years at Athens College one year after the college had restored itself in Benaki Hall. You were ten, and you spent the next eight years as a boarder.

Your mother now lived in a hotel, where you spent weekends with her.

At Athens College, students formed opposing armies to fight over you for your delicate beauty, and you, in a cubicle of the toilet which was the only place you could be alone, wept.

You found, one day, a worm in the cabbage soup that was served in the dining hall, and refused to eat. You were not allowed to get up from your seat until you did, and sat for hours, insisting you wouldn't eat, but finally did, because you must.

The one person you talked to was the young man who kept the pigs in the pigsty on the grounds of the college. He told you about sex.

You cut your wrists, wanting to die, knowing you would not.

Your mother gave you a gold sovereign to spend as you wished. You said you wanted to buy a painting from the teacher of art at the college, and, the sovereign in your hand, scrutinized carefully the paintings in the studio, all on wood panel because canvas was unprocurable. You chose a portrait of a boy who, during the war, lived in the streets, stealing food as he could and begging.

On October 16, 1949, Radio Free Greece, the Communist radio station, announced the end of Communist fighting.

The Communist Party was outlawed, and the death penalty was imposed for members.

In school, Thucydides' history of the Peloponnesian War was required reading—a war that lasted twenty-six years and ended with the defeat of Athens.

In that war, fathers killed their sons, men were dragged from the temples they'd sought refuge in or were butchered on the altars; some were walled up in the temples to die there. Those who could, killed themselves in the temples; some hanged themselves from trees to escape worse than simply being killed.

It seemed to you that Greek history was so often a history of defeat.

As you considered yourself a refugee from Constantinople, you lived, as if within your lifetime, the defeat of Byzantium when, on May 29, 1453, the forces of Sultan Mohamet II broke through the walls and Constantinople fell. The gutters of the streets, strewn with icons and sacred chalices sacked from churches, ran with blood, and Emperor Constantine XI Palaeologus Dragases was lost, lost forever, having thrown himself among his soldiers to stop a breach. All that was found of him was a sock embroidered with the eagle of the imperial insignia.

Even in the glory of Greek independence from the Ottomans in 1823, you knew that, as in every glory, there was defeat.

Taken with classmates to Constantinople to visit the Patriarchate in the old Phanariot quarter, Turkish boys threw stones at you all. On a bus, your buttocks were pinched by an elderly Turk.

Your first sexual experience, even before you knew of self masturbation, was in a cinema, where an elderly man sitting next to you unzipped your trousers and masturbated you. Totally bemused, you left the cinema, your boy's penis still out.

Your mother gave you extra allowance, which you knew from your schoolmates, who had also been given extra allowances, was to go to a certain woman, an elderly professional, whom parents trusted to bring their sons into manhood, generations of sons. You went to her, the last of your schoolmates, and she, from experience, understood, and merely put a hand on your shoulder and after a short while told you to go join your friends.

Through continuing correspondence with the mother of Herr Werner, your mother arranged for you to go to Germany to study German, as you wanted so to do. On your way, you stopped in Venice, your first time there. You took photographs at odd angles, inspired by the photographs of Rodchenko. All money gone, you had to wire your mother for more. The summer was spent in Frankfurt, with a German-speaking family, with a boy your age who said he longed to go to Greece, where the orange trees grow.

On your return to Athens, a sudden view of the Acropolis and the Parthenon over the city made you think, as if for the first time, of what the meaning was to you, a Greek.

These memorized lines by Shelley, from *Hellas,* suddenly had deep meaning:
*Another Athens shall arise,*
*And to a remoter time*
*Bequeath, like sunset to the skies,*
*The splendour of its prime.*

On a school excursion to Epidaurus, you stood in the center of the ancient amphitheater and, arms raised, recited the poem by the Italian-born Greek poet Solomos, in which Athena rises from the sea.

You wrote poetry, in Greek and English, on the back of mimeographed forms outlining the responsibilities of the General Surveillant, who, during his period of surveillance, "is the one person who is principally and generally responsible for what goes on in the School and among the boys."

Unhappy at Athens College, by the age of seventeen you had made up your mind to become the leading student of your year, and you did. You were awarded the Annual Howland Prize for a speaking contest. You became a General Surveillant Officer for the younger students, and also a Table Monitor, insisting the younger students finish all the food on their plates.

Among your early collection of books were the poems, in Greek, of Mayakovsky, with an introduction by Stalin, praising the poet as the greatest and the most socialist of Soviet poets ever, not mentioning that the poet had killed himself. Also, you had various pamphlets by Mao Tse-tung, one, *On Contradiction,* with sentences underlined.

You became a member of the outlawed Communist Party, and you recruited other members to the Party.

As head of the student council of Athens College, you held the key to the room where the mimeograph machine was kept locked, and, at 3:00 a.m., you would go from your bed in the dormitory down to the room, mimeograph Communist propaganda, and, on evenings off, would go into cinemas in Athens and from balconies throw down the sheets into the auditorium, then run.

You translated Stephen Spender's
*O YOUNG MEN O YOUNG COMRADES*
*Ω ΝΕΟΙ ΑΝΘΡΩΠΟΙ Ω ΝΕΟΙ ΣΥΝΤΡΟΦΟΙ*


Visiting your mother on weekends, you would, when she was
out, hide the propaganda behind a bookshelf. Once, on retrieving
the propaganda, you found that the flap of the envelope you had put
them in had been left open, a sign of your mother's awareness of
what you were doing, but she never mentioned the propaganda to
you, nor did you to her. At the least, if discovered, you would have
been arrested, imprisoned, and interrogated.


You made a list, chronologically ordered, of the philosophers
whose works you studied: Descartes (1596–1690), Spinoza (1632–
1677), Leibniz (1646–1716), Kant (1724–1804), Fichte (1762–1814),
Hegel (1770–1831), Schopenhauer (1788–1860), Nietzsche (1844–
1900), Comte (1798–1857), Spencer (1820–1903).


Essential to your education was music. You listened carefully
to a musette by Bach to transcribe the notes. You wrote your own
composition, *ΕΞΑΥΛΩΣΙΣ*, but crossed it out, not good enough.


You wrote extensive essays on the Rhapsodies (*ΡΑΨΩΔΙΕΣ*) of
the Odyssey, to the admiration of your teacher.


You wrote an essay, *Πάτροκλος* (*Patroclus*) in which "Ο Αχιλλέας,
ο Αχιλλέας" ("Achilles, Achilles") appears often.

And in a school notebook with mottled green covers, you wrote an essay on the Byzantine philosopher George Gemistus Plethon, who was, you argued, the founder of the Italian Renaissance, having brought Plato to the attention of the Italians.

On your commencement, you gave the valedictory speech and were criticized by starting off your speech with music by Shostakovich.

At a Communist cell meeting, your poetry was criticized for being too formalistic, and, moreover, too sexually ambiguous. You would not submit to an ideal and insisted on the total freedom of your poetry, and you left the Party.

From Athens College, you would remember a stark classroom with an icon of Christ above a blackboard with geometrical figures in chalk. You would remember glass-fronted cabinets filled with trophy cups. You would remember narrow beds, a blanket folded neatly at the foot of each.

# Beta

*Grief makes the griever believe the death of his lover is unique.*
*Grief demands a grand, timeless expression, and the bereaved tries,*
*tries for that expression, and wonders if the expression is false.*

After graduation from Athens College, you went to America—
first to Denison in Ohio, then Wesleyan in Connecticut, then Harvard in Cambridge, Massachusetts—to continue your studies. You
did not want to be a doctor.

At Denison, where you were a Fulbright student, you wrote essays on *Beowulf*, Sir Thomas Brown, John Bunyan, Isaac Walton,
John Donne, Byron, Wordsworth, Browning, Walt Whitman. A
comment on your essay on Walt Whitman by your professor: "For
heaven's sake, develop your criticism along well-tried academic
paths before you try to express your soul."

Your first summer in America, after the scholastic year at Denison, you worked in a meat-packing factory, wearing a white cap and
smock. You wrote to your mother in Athens how proud you were to
have a proletarian job in capitalist America.

You wrote stories and poems, some published in the literary
magazine of Denison, *Exiles:*

*He stood up naked from his bed and looked at his body in the mirror hanging on the wall across from him. He was searching for the ancient beauty of his ancestors.*

*I was walking through the streets, thinking of his red shirt.*

*Going from the Mediterranean to the Atlantic, starting from Greece, where the color is light blue. In Italy the blue is deeper. In France, clear blue. In Spain, the sea is intense, like a kiss. Gibraltar: the colors blue, green, gray, violet. His eyes had this color.*

After graduating from Denison, awarded your BA, you went to Wesleyan for your MA. You attended a reading given by W. H. Auden at a fraternity, and, to the chagrin of the brotherhood, you asked Auden to comment on the opinion that the quality of his poetry had declined in recent years.

During the summer, you worked in a Greek resort in the Catskill Mountains, and every weekend a Greek gentleman from New York arrived with gifts for you.

From Wesleyan you went to Harvard to continue studies in philosophy. Your final examination included such questions as: "Compare in some detail Locke's, Berkeley's, and Hume's uses of the term 'idea.' What, according to these philosophers, are the roles of ideas in human knowledge, including perception, knowledge of causes and substances, self-knowledge, and knowledge of necessary truth?"

You had stayed up all night, on NoDoz, to study for this examination, but got the date wrong, a day too early, so when the day did come you, in a daze, failed.

On your return to Greece, you had to do your military service, and were sent to boot camp in Tripolis, in the middle of the Peloponnesus. You had your head shaved by a local barber before you went so you wouldn't suffer that humiliation. Ordered to wash a floor, you turned your will to washing it so well it was like new.

Demobbed, you became friendly with writers, among them Andreas Emberikos (whose short stories you eventually translated into English) and Nanos Valaoritis and Costas Tachsis, with whom you formed a group that met each week in a coffeehouse and, with you as one of the editors, started a literary magazine, Πάλι (*Again*), in which you published your first poems in Greek.

The old painter Yannis Tsarouchis, who was a friend, painted tough young men with butterfly wings. He gave you a jam jar painted with naked youths, in which you kept pencils.

And you made friends—oh, no doubt in part because of your youth and beauty—with an elderly diplomat who introduced you to the world of diplomats.

On your first visit to London, you were in the entourage of Queen Frederika and invited to a reception for her at Buckingham Palace, about which you were ironical—Greek diplomacy had a tradition of supporting Greek poets, however undiplomatic they were.

In 1965, you moved from Athens to London to work in the Press Office of the Greek embassy. Nanos Valaoritis gave you a list of people in the literary world whom he had known when he lived

in London, among them the poet Stephen Spender, whose poetry
you had translated when a student and whom you admired for his
vision of compassionate politics. You came to live in London with
the desire—not the fantasy, for desire in you was distinct from
fantasy—to meet someone with whom you would live and fulfill
your life. You were now twenty-eight.

You knew you would never win. Freed, therefore, of ambition,
you stubbornly did everything to the best of your ability.

# Gamma

*Though grief knows in grief's longing this is not true to the reality of the lost lover, grief will surround him with universal beauty.*

We could have met in Boston. At seventeen, I had been a boarder at Boston College for my freshman year in 1957, the same year, you, at twenty-one, had been at Harvard, working on your doctorate, a thesis on Nietzsche as poet, and living in a rented room in Cambridge. You had had a job in the foreign language bookshop Schoenhof's, in Harvard Square, where I would often go if only to be at the center of cross-cultural foreignness. Did I once buy a book from you, thinking you the beautiful foreigner whom I fantasized meaning so much to me?

In Boston, I fantasized often about Greece. I discovered, in a secondhand bookshop on Beacon Hill, the poetry of Trumbull Stickney, a late nineteenth-century New Englander, a Yankee, who lived most of his life in Paris and who loved Greece. Trumbull Stickney wrote of a prize-winning singer "who danced by Victory's torchlight, glistening-limbed, his body wet with music, the ivies black plaited in his honey-hair, and his lithe skin laughing with the subtle fire of blood." He wrote sonnets: "From Greece," "Sunium," "Mt. Lykaion," "Near Helikon," "Eleusis," "Mt. Ida."

This, from Trumbull Stickney, described my efforts at love:
*I thought the perfect end of love was peace*
*Over the long-forgiven sufferings.*
*But something else, I know not what it is,*

*The words that come so nearly and then not,*
*The vanity, the error of the whole,*
*The strong cross-purpose, oh, I know not what*
*Cries dreadfully in the distracted soul.*

In my unhappiness, I read and reread Plato's *Symposium,* which aroused such fantasies of ideal Greece in me for affirming that "love is some sort of desire," desire made whole and fulfilled.

But among Stickney's Greek poems I found one, *Oneiropolos,* about an Indian in ancient Athens, who, in the shadow of a wall in the Agora, deserted because of the noonday heat, talks to his companion, Sakhi, about his now-dead master Brihadashua, "pure and charitable, who dwelt in Kashi by the holy stream," whom he so misses, for he finds Athens "a dying town filled of a feeble race, small of their all-expressing tongue, dancers and frolickers, philosophers drunken and sense-tied to the trembling world."

All I knew about you before we met—given by a friend in Boston your name and address and telephone number in London, where I planned to stop on my way to fantasy Athens to try to find a job teaching there—was that you were Greek. On my arrival in London, aged twenty-five and open to the world, I telephoned you and you invited me to tea. But when I rang your bell, 6 Wyndham Place, no one answered. I thought I'd got the time wrong, so that June afternoon I walked for an hour in Hyde Park, then back to your street door and rang again, and now you opened.

When I first saw you opening your door to me!

You wore a brown cardigan and gray trousers, and there seemed to me to be nothing in your apartment that was Greek, but modern pictures on the walls by British artists I had not heard of. Your voice was soft but very clear. You asked me about myself, and hardly responded to my asking about you.

You showed me a large book of etchings by David Hockney, inspired by the poems of Constantine Cavafy, poems, included in the book, which you had translated and were lightly edited by Stephen Spender, whom you said you knew. Many of the etchings were of naked young men delineated in delicate lines.

The sitting room became dim as the hours passed, and when you asked if I would join you for dinner, I, in a trance from your attention, said, as an American does, "Sure." In your bedroom, you changed and emerged dressed in a white suit, a pink shirt, and a wide tie, gray with large black polka dots. In the taxi to the restaurant—the Idelweiss—you told me you were not rich, as if to clarify this. And, as if to justify politically your clothes, you said the Soviet ambassador approved of Carnaby Street and the King's Road, where yellow bell-bottomed trousers and red velvet jackets and long multicolored scarves were sold, because the style came from the proletariat.

And I said, "Sure," when you asked me back to your apartment.

Our first night together, we could have been the inspiration of a poem by Cavafy, who would have noted the yellow satin counterpane you pulled from your bed before we got into it together.

But you would not make love. You wanted to lie with me and talk. I, who only really knew promiscuity, didn't understand, but you said you must first know a person before making love. You believed lovemaking was a long and intimate conversation. *That* conversation with you was filled with the delicacy of your sensuality, for sensuality and sensitivity were in you one, έρως καί αγάπη, eros and agape.

You asked to see me again. I was staying with a former lover, my first lover, Öçi, a Hungarian-Greek brought up in Turkey, whom I had met in Spain some five years before and whom I had come to see in London, where he now lived. Öçi did not like my seeing you, but, yes, I wanted to. I began to spend nights with you, in your bed.

You invited me to a recital by Rostropovich in Festival Hall, and afterward suggested we walk to Trafalgar Square, across the then-pedestrian side of Hungerford Bridge. You threw a copper penny into the Thames, and I asked why. You said, "For luck." And in Trafalgar Square, on a stone bench in a corner and in full view of an illuminated, gushing fountain, you told me you were in love with an elderly Englishman, now away, but would end that relationship. You said I was the reason, but I must not feel anything but that I had helped you make a choice. Then you made me promise I would be totally honest—for dishonesty would make everything go wrong—and asked me if I would live with you. Swaying back and forth, I said yes. And you smiled.

Later you told me you had seen me outside the door ringing someone's bell, but, you thought, not yours, for no bell rang for you. You saw me leave, and, on an impulse, went out to check if your bell rang. It didn't. You repaired it, and, having seen me through the sheer curtain over the front window, you regretted the mishappening. You were surprised that I came back. You said you wouldn't have.

Your bed became our bed.

The idea of a thing infuses the thing with more than the thing is—the idea of our bed.

In rudimentary Greek, I wrote a song:
Πού είναι η αγάπη μου;
Νάτος! Είναι στο κρεβάτι μου!
(Where is my Love?
There! He's in my bed!)

I had a breakdown soon after we began to live together, as though, now secure in you, I could let go, and let go I did, in fits of howling. Left too weak to get to the bathroom after an all-night fit, you helped me, an arm about my waist to steady me. I slept for days, you watching over me. With strength enough that I could now go out, we walked through Hyde Park. You stayed close by me, calmly telling me at moments of convulsing fear, "Breathe in deeply, then breathe out," and, "Be still, be still." At home, you lay beside me on our bed, an arm over me till I went still. You cured me.

Our Saturday afternoon naps, all chores, including shopping, done, we shut off the telephone, closed the curtains of our room, undressed, and got into bed, our arms held out to each other.

Making love, we were beyond desire: we *had* each other.

To be beyond desire in making love!

To be among those, as Stickney longed to be, "who love too much to think of love"!

Awake beside you in our bed as you slept, the bedroom dim, I, looking at you, would think: Is it possible that anyone so beautiful can be my lover?

In our making love, your beauty awed me so when, drawing back from kissing me, you smiled, and I reached out to bring you back. Why, with you, should I ever want to make love with someone else?

You wrote strange poems about our lovemaking:
*You moved your arm under my neck*
*Your lips touched burning on my shoulder*
*I dreamt of sinking into seas*
*Dangerous seas*
*High seas*
*Black seas*
*The sea of serenity*
*The sea that separates*
*The cold sea.*

You wrote "surreal" poems about me in our first year: "The helicopters of his hair," "The syringe of his open mouth," "The train that thunders on his back," and "His breath embroiders me."

Your work at the Press Office required you to read many newspapers and cut out all articles in which Greece was referred to. The country was in a bad way, the royal family, you said, sending money to banks abroad in preparation for their having to leave. Closed in among themselves, they spoke German. There was no true Greek aristocracy.

While you were at the Press Office, I wrote stories, which you read and commented on, the first person I had ever known to take me seriously as a writer.

Alone, I sometimes fantasized making love with someone else, which you told me you never did because you would not be engaged in fantasy.

What was our future together, two young men who, in love with each other, would have no progeny, no generation upon generation of our same-sex love? Was there anything in our same-sex love to bring reason to it, or only the experience beyond reason and inexplicable? Is there something tragic in the love of one man for another if, in fact, love survives against having no progeny but centered in itself, a mutual possession, a suicide pact in that love is fated to end in love?

Our first Christmas together, we dressed in suits and ties and went to midnight mass at the Brompton Oratory, where, standing behind a porphyry pillar and hearing the Latin chant and breathing in the incense, I felt we were both as removed from the world outside as if we were in ancient Rome, and I felt in you the happiness of that removal. Back in 6 Wyndham Place, we lit candles on a decorated tree, and we were in our home.

I learned about you: you were not sentimental, but the sight of an old woman in a crowd alone carrying a small valise was unbearable to you and made tears rise into your eyes; you were not ever exuberantly happy, your laughter light; you were not passionate but tender, not spontaneous but measured; you did not like receiving gifts, and you would not accept gratitude for a favor; you had close friends but were not social; you could not tell a joke that was funny.

I recorded, in the back pages of an agenda, a conversation I had with you after I said I wanted to be like you:
Laughing: "Me? You mustn't be like me."
"Why?"

"Don't you know me enough to see?"

"I mustn't know you at all, then, because I do want to take after you."

"In what way?"

"Be, like you, determined."

Laughter again: "Determined about what?"

"To do what you don't want to do."


And:

You: "I had a friend once, an American."

I, suddenly jealous: "An American?"

"Yes."

"You never told me about him."

"No, I never did."

"Was he a lover?"

"I loved him, if that's what you mean. I don't know if he loved me. He was older than I."

"How much older?"

"I don't know—fifteen, twenty years."

"That much older?"

Laughing lightly: "He said to me once, you're nothing. He called me Mr. Nothing."

"What!"

"Why does that shock you?"

"Because it does." I became angry. "Who was this stupid man?"

"It doesn't matter."

"I want to know."

"It doesn't matter."

You carrying one red rose, we made a pilgrimage to Highgate to see the tomb of Karl Marx, a massive bronze head on a plinth, at the bottom of which you placed the rose. You were silent, and I silent with you.

The first time I was unfaithful, I, young, met a young man on a bus as I was going home, and you were in your office, away from home. I told you after—excited more in telling you than in the sex—and you, upset, asked, "In our bed?"

Sometimes I wished that you would be unfaithful to me, which, I fantasized, would excite me. Then, when I was away and you were unfaithful and on my return told me, I raged.

Once, when we were making love, you pinched my nipples hard, which hurt so I told you to stop (pain played no part in our lovemaking). I wondered if this little act of violence was spontaneous, emerging from your feelings towards me.

The bed's a battlefield, the old lady said. You accepted my infidelity, and more as they occurred, but I didn't accept yours. I wouldn't sleep. "Let's sleep," you'd say, "let's sleep." You reached an arm across me as I lay rigid, separate, and you drew me to your body, where I gave in to sleeping close to you, our sleeping close together a resolution, beyond our understanding, so that we woke at peace.

Making love, I wished I could press my body entirely into yours, move as you moved, think as you thought, feel as you felt.

Sometimes, after making love, I thought we'd finally die together, there where we fell asleep together.

You and I, in turn, would say, as we together fell asleep, "Wouldn't it be wonderful if we never woke?" A joke?

You said to me, "I'll die before you," and I to you, "No, I'll die first."

As if wanting to die, you said you longed to return to Greece and live in a mountain village in Epirus, attending to your animals, your cats, your dogs, your goats, your donkeys, your cows, and your geese. Wanting not to be left out, I said, "We'll die there together."

However insecure I made you by our rows, rows that made me sometimes think we must separate, our making love together when, after all, we were in bed together, always made you laugh with the relief of security reassured, as if the rows and any threat of separation had never occurred.

Our rows! Almost all of them had to do with your need for order. Though I was orderly too (and a friend told us that what made it possible for us to live together domestically was that we were both orderly), your need for order was far in excess of mine. You complained if, in the bathroom, I let soap in the soap dish become slimy, if in flossing my teeth I speckled the mirror, if I squeezed the toothpaste tube from the middle, if I did not lower the seat of the toilet bowl, if I did not hang the bath mat over the rim of the tub, if

I did not turn on or off the light by the little wooden knob at the end of the cord but by the cord, if, if, if, oh, if I replaced the roll of toilet paper so that it rolled outwardly rather than inwardly against the wall. You would not listen when a friend told you that he had been in ducal houses, even princely house, where the toilet paper was always rolled outwardly. I tried to be amused by your fastidiousness, but, complaining against your complaints, shouted that I would not have our lives reduced to minutia. You shouted back, "I will not live in bedlam." And you never, ever apologized, as if constitutionally opposed to apology.

Whenever, after a row, I said, "We must sit down together and talk about this to resolve it," you would insist, "No, we're not going to talk about it." A day would be spent in silence, and then, suddenly, you would embrace me, and I would think, loving me as I know he does, he's right not to talk about problems.

Our lovemaking resolved everything for you, and then, seeing such peace come to you, peace came to me. Our lovemaking had that deep, deep meaning for us both, so much so that, during a row, I'd think: We'll make love, then sleep together, and everything will be all right.

You'd turn to bless me just before we'd settled down, deep in our bed, to sleep, and, sleeping, fall from layer upon layer to the darkness, where all was forgiven.

Woken at night by the ringing telephone, you panicked, as if woken by a siren warning of bombs.

What happened in our sleep that all the conflicts were resolved there? As mysterious as the Eleusinian Mysteries, the lost ritual that granted to the initiates a happy life beyond the grave, something entranced us. I holding you or you holding me, we entered into the temple of such secrets that they were kept from us when we woke from them.

You became so attached to the objects of our home—cheap pieces of furniture we bought when, with very little to spend, we began our domestic lives together—they became fetishes, so you would never replace the cheap furniture with better, never, and never, never our bed!

To love, you believed you must love purely, which was to love free of all the transitory, free of the relative, free of history, which was to love, oh, absolutely. So you must love me by finding in me the center of love absolute. And this you did—kept the center fixed in all its purity—though you suffered my vicissitudes, my infidelities, my crude history, my impurity.

After years together, many years, you asked, "How many times have we made love?" Our lovemaking was deepening into sleep. "Ten thousand times? More?" "More," I answered, "than we've made love with any other, much, much more." You laughed, reassured by this, and asked, "Into infinity?" Laughing, too, I said, "Infinity."

In her biography of her father, the Byzantine emperor Alexius I, Anna Comnena wrote, "Yours and mine, let these cruel words never be said between us," a line quoted by Cavafy in a poem.

# Delta

*Grief cannot help but idealize.*     | 43

In London—surrounded by many English friends—we lived in a Greek world.

The first Greek I learned was to call you my Love in your language: Αγάπη μου.

The first Greek poem you taught me was one of Sappho's, in which she sleeps alone, *Εγω δέ μόνα κατεύδω.*

You told me I always got whatever Greek I spoke wrong: I could never get the genders straight.

I wondered sometimes if your Greekness meant more to me than it did to you.

I imagined you, on your father's side, in the provincial ancient town of Apollonia. As a young man, you would perhaps have longed to be in Athens, and, hearing about them, have envied the Athenians of your age, the ephebi, in the Panathenian festival, carrying an image of Athens to be washed in the sea at Phaleron, and then, in a torch-lit procession, returning with her to the Acropolis, in some ribaldry.

And on your mother's side, in Constantinople at the height of the Christian Byzantine Empire, you would perhaps have fantasized, not about Athens, by then itself a dusty provincial town, but about Rome—for your mother was, far back in the history of Rome's displacement to Byzantium, Roman—where you would have been freer in your manners and your moods than within strict Byzantine formalities. You might have longed to be in degenerate Rome.

Could I ever understand your Greekness? Not the yellowing marbles, not the cicadas in the cypress trees, not even the bright blue sea—none of these, which you yourself rejected as merely picturesque, defined you as Greek.

That you were Greek inspired in me such a sense of honor for all the high principles you yourself aspired to, and yet you made me see, in the midst of those principles, a hoplite in Piraeus haggling with a manufacturer over the cost of a shield.

You characterized Greeks as pompously self-righteous, argumentative, and slightly ridiculous.

I would have been considered to ancient Greeks a barbarian. I would have done everything to learn the language, recite the poetry, take on the cultivated manners, but I would never have been invited to a symposium or allowed into the Assembly, as you would have been.

For you to feel our domestic lives were complete we needed: olive oil, olives, lemons, grapes, and Greek mountain tea, φασκόμιλο.

We observed Greek Easter. We went to Moscow Road each Orthodox Easter time to buy the makings of *mageritsa,* livers and kidneys and other innards and masses of fresh dill, the soup to be eaten on return home from the midnight resurrection together with the brioche, *tsoureki,* that had red eggs baked into it, for Moscow Road is where, in London, the Greek Orthodox cathedral is, and Greek restaurants and grocery shops are. Walking, we passed a cheap hotel, 16 Queensborough Terrace, on which a blue plaque stated Constantine Cavafy had stayed there long before we were born.

Philolaus wrote that we are born attuned to the music of the spheres but do not hear it, as coppersmiths, so accustomed to the noise of the smithy, do not hear the noise. How, he asked, can the sun and the moon and all the stars, so great in number and in size and moving so rapidly, not produce a sound immensely great? And as the speeds of the heavenly bodies are in the same ratios as musical concordances, the sound given forth by the circular movement of the sun and moon and stars is a harmony. This music, heard but unheard, is to us like music. And Philolaus thought: a soul is in a kind of attunement, a harmony. And I think: our souls were attuned to each other.

# Epsilon

*Grief reveals the griever's vanity, the vanity of his grief, the vanity of all his life.*

The person you loved in London was the poet Stephen Spender, who when you and I met was away, in residence at the Library of Congress in Washington, from where he sent you missives. One, a reproduction of Andrea Del Castagno's *The Youthful David,* you took as a sign of his knowing about us before I met him.

You showed me a poem he had written and sent to you—he in a rage of longing for your presence, willing your name be flesh on the blank, unanswering page.

You wanted me to meet him on his return to London, but you must speak to him first, so I walked about Hyde Park for an hour and on my return met Stephen. I was awkward, and said I hoped I would see him again, and he, a large man in a rumpled suit, said he hoped so too. You showed him out, and I heard him say, "I like your friend."

Stephen introduced us into the English world around us. Through him, we met the last of Bloomsbury in E.M. Forster (the friend of

Constantine Cavafy!) and Duncan Grant and Dadie Reylands and
Angelica Garnett and John Lehmann, and we heard him talk of
Virginia and Leonard Woolf and T.S. Eliot. I am left with memories
of the people we met in that world, and you and I in it, sometimes
imagining it our world.

Stephen, alone with us for supper, mentioned that he was to go
to the south of France to plant trees in the garden of his and his wife
Natasha's house. You suggested I go with him to help. Stephen was
enthusiastic. A gardener planted the trees as Stephen and I looked
on. Returned to London, I asked, after all, why you had suggested I
go alone with Stephen, and you replied, "To test you." I never asked
you to explain, as I never asked you to explain your relationship
with Stephen.

We were both foreigners in England. And yet, all our dearest
friends were English, as if we had in them repudiated our separate
countries, so we spent weekends with these English friends in the
Wiltshire countryside and took walks along rough paths and over
stiles in gumboots against the puddles and the mud, then back to
tea, assimilated into this country, not ours.

Not our country, yet our friendships in England helped extend
us into the world. Returning to our home from an evening with our
dear friend Julia Hodgkin, we felt, sitting side by side in the London
taxi, a sense of satisfaction, accomplishment even, that we together
should have such a loving friend, such loving friends.

An elderly woman at a drinks party (her husband recently dead) said to me, "You may not believe it now, but if you and Nikos stay together and age together, the signs of age—wrinkles and brown spots and a sagging chin—will make you love him all the more."

Natasha Spender invited both of us to Saint Jerome, their house in the south of France. You helped her in the garden while Stephen and I read on the terrace. She packed a wicker picnic basket for an excursion to the Ardèche Gorge, where we sat about a rug spread out on a large flat rock by the river. People were swimming in the river, carried along by the current, and from among them rose three naked youths, their long locks dripping, who lay in the sunlight before us on the smooth rock. Embarrassed for her, you hurriedly helped Natasha repack the picnic basket, and I saw Stephen, smiling, take from his shirt pocket his spectacles to stare at the naked youths.

Whenever Natasha was to be away, she would ring and ask us: please look after Stephen.

You couldn't have been more centered in the English world than in your being invited to join the Cranium Club, a dining club established by Bloomsbury, where you met the last of the Garnetts, the Keyneses, the Trevelyans. The club had the distinction of having blackballed T.S. Eliot as being too boring. I was not invited to join.

You were asked to be on the board of the Institute of Contemporary Arts, but after a few meetings suggested that the institute be shut. You resigned.

I was the social one, you the one who wanted always to stay at home with your cats, with music and books and our collection of paintings. You wanted me, too, to stay at home with you, but also allowed that I would go away for a country weekend. You never limited me to what you wanted of me.

Yet you enjoyed, as much as you enjoyed any occasion, supper parties we gave for friends. I look through old date books at the many names of friends who came, and think: he's dead, she's dead, they're dead. You always insisted on doing the clearing up before we went to bed.

We were invited to dine by an aristocratic lady, a Grecophile, who admired you. She also invited an aged woman of the high gentry. The big public subject, debated in Parliament, was the banning of fox hunting with dogs, which you were in favor of. The woman of high gentry said, "I accept your feelings, Nikos, but you must understand that I grew up with fox hunting and find it difficult to shift to your point of view, acceptable as your point of view is." You wouldn't accept this, and went on and on, condemning, more and more vehemently, the sport. You destroyed the evening, and on our way home I reproached you. "Don't tell me what I can and can't say," you said. The aristocratic lady, who admired you very much, invited us again with the woman of very high gentry, and this time you were impressed by the work she did for prisoners—helping them earn a little money by selling crafts, such as weaving, embroidery, tassel-making, that they were able to practice in prison—and the evening was a success. You were not ingratiating to anyone of the upper class, to anyone rich, or to anyone famous, as I was.

We often went to Paris for exhibitions in the Grand Palais, including one of the exhibitions of Courbet. In London at a dinner party, you said that Courbet is a great painter, and objected to a woman, another guest, when she said she didn't like Courbet. You said, "You can't not like Courbet." This startled her, and you startled her even more when, after she stood by her rights to have an opinion, you said, "You don't have the right. Opinions are irrelevant, and especially irrelevant to the greatness of Courbet."

You believed it was impossible to say about a person, I dislike or even I like him or her, for a person is too complex to be limited by any opinion one might have. And yet you would say, "She's wonderful!"

Returning home one evening from your office, you said, "Let's move to Australia." And I, "But we don't know anything about Australia." You retorted, "You have no imagination."

The painter R.B. Kitaj and his beautiful wife, Sandra Fisher, also a painter, came to supper. You and I had a little row, I can't remember about what, but, jesting because you would not tolerate bickering, I accused you of being the difficult one, and you accused me of being the difficult one while I insisted I was the easy one. Sandra said, "I thought it would be different, two men living together." Kitaj grunted. They are both dead.

Perhaps only in London could you be the cosmopolitan Greek you were. You couldn't in Athens, for in Athens you were a refugee, and, as a refugee, must contend with a culture, though Greek, that was not yours. In London, where you avoided Greeks, your Greek-ness was yours essentially, yours purely. In London, you were more attractively Greek to the English than I was American, for I was not classical, as you were.

Our second year together, dictators took over Greece and you left your job at the Greek embassy. We moved from the luxury flat in Wyndham Place, West One, to a small apartment in Battersea, South West Eleven. We painted walls, hung pictures, built book-shelves and cupboards, bought and borrowed furniture, our only heating a paraffin stove, and for pets two Burmese cats.

You saw in London many Greek refugees from the dictatorship, some of whom stayed with us.

Not British, your first language not English, with no experience in publishing, you became, after an interview with the founder, a commissioning editor for poetry at Penguin Books. Your position at Penguin Books put you at a center of literary life in London. You reintroduced in publication such poets as F.T. Prince, John Heath Stubbs, David Gascoyne, and introduced such new poets as Lee Harwood, Harry Fainlight, and, then unpublished in England, John Ashbery.

Some poets became dependent on you. You were called by the police to come to a station to rescue the visionary poet David Gas-coyne, who had been arrested trying to get into Buckingham Palace to warn the queen of a conspiracy to kill her.

You gave money to young poets, first asking my permission.

Your favorite expression in praising the work of a poet, painter, composer: "It's so innovative!"

For his birthday, you gave to the young son of friends scores of Beethoven sonatas, which the boy, not having seen them before, propped on his piano and played, to everyone's exclamation. Calmly, you said to him, "You have a lot of practicing to do."

You said to me about my writing, "Don't disappoint me."

You insisted we *must* go see the production of a play at the Old Vic by a director I had never heard of; we *must* go to Wigmore Hall for a recital by a pianist I had never heard of; we *must* go to an exhibition at the Tate by artists I had never heard of. I was always amazed at what you knew and how you knew so much.

When you moved from Penguin Books—because, after the death of the founder, you saw that the publishing house was selling out the standards you had admired it for—to the independent Thames & Hudson, you became a publisher of books on artists by art historians. Many of these books won awards, which I then assumed you ostentatiously had no interest in. At a dinner party to celebrate the success of one of these books, you, when complimented, raised a napkin to cover your face, as if to absent yourself. At the time, I thought you were trying to impress more with your absence than your presence, but I was wrong, for you always thought of yourself as more absent than present.

You went to the Soviet Union to commission books, among the first publishers to do so, and you returned with a lapel button of the head of Lenin.

On your return to the Soviet Union, I went with you. We had KGB minders, the one in Leningrad a young man who dominated a meeting between you and art historians in the Hermitage. The art historians were intimidated by him and hardly spoke. He left briefly, perhaps to make a telephone call, and while he was away, you said, "I can't stand him," which, in a whisper, was translated by one of the art historians to the others, and they all smiled, rather tight smiles. If you had been a Soviet, you would have been very intolerant of authority.

When the Soviet Union fell apart, you, always a believer, said, "That Communism didn't work in the USSR does not mean Communism can't work elsewhere." And you added, "The great fault of Soviet Communism, which was a kind of religion, is that, as a true religion should, it did not forgive."

One of the founding historians of Byzantium, who believed that Byzantium was one of the great periods in history, Steven Runciman, was often a guest to supper, and loved you, I imagined, because he saw in you that you were Byzantine. (He told us anecdotes that widened our London world so much into his we were with him playing piano duets with the last emperor of China, Henry Pu-Yi.) You were, he said, to inherit from him a bronze cockerel because you loved the hens he kept on the estate of his castle in Scotland. I wanted him to love me as he loved you, but he looked away from me.

You commissioned Runciman to write a book on Mistra, the Byzantine city in the Peloponnese, the center from which the Byzantine philosopher George Gemistus Plethon taught, and I recalled an essay you wrote on Plethon when you were at Athens College. So admired in Italy, Plethon was invited, in 1438, to Ferrara, and from Ferrara to Florence, where he gave lectures on Plato, and was called by Marsiglio Picino "the second Plato." In Plethon's honor, Cosimo de' Medici founded the Academy at Florence.

When my first novel, *The Ghost of Henry James,* was published, you invited friends to a Greek taverna in London, where I smashed glasses against the floor. You paid the bill for all of us, and for the smashed glasses. In our apartment, kneeling before the toilet vomiting, I exclaimed, "I'm so happy!" but what I meant was that I knew you were happy for me, happy for me at a depth that you would never be happy for yourself.

And while you supported me in my writing, you wrote your poems and put them in a drawer of your desk, your longest called "Pure Reason." You also kept on translating the poetry of Constantine Cavafy, your translations both clear-minded and sensual, delicately clear-minded and delicately sensual, as if you translated him into yourself, making of his beautiful white flowers, his colored handkerchiefs, his mirror hanging in the front hall reflecting the face of a beautiful youth, objects from your life, objects that subtly inspire the pensive, and the senses too.

R.B. Kitaj's portrait of you, in a large blue overcoat walking past a provocative girl in a transparent skirt through which her pubis shows, your eyes, with wire-framed spectacles, looking down contemplatively, while, behind, Kitaj himself descends the steep staircase of a whorehouse, is meant to refer to Cavafy contemplating, in lonely isolation, the passing pleasures of the flesh.

W.H. Auden, who from time to time came to supper in our small apartment with Stephen, liked you for standing up to him. Commenting on the dictatorship in Greece, he said, "Look, Nikos, Greece was best run, an efficient country, under the Turks," to which you said, "Nonsense," as no one else seemed ever to have done. Auden also said about Cavafy, "His love poems are kitsch, really," to which you said nothing, perhaps, after all, agreeing.

In London, you gave a lecture on Cavafy and emphatically made his homosexuality central to his vision. Stephen and Natasha Spender were in the front row of the audience.

In your talk on Constantine Cavafy at the London Hellenic Society, you gave his history: born in Alexandria, Egypt, in 1863, to a Constantinopolitan family, his childhood spent in England, London and Liverpool, his adolescence in Constantinople, his adulthood in Alexandria, which he thereafter hardly left. His first visit to Greece was in 1901, when he was thirty-eight years old, during which he kept a flat, dutiful diary in English. His only other visit to Greece was when he was seventy, for medical reasons: a tracheotomy for cancer of the throat. He returned to Alexandria, where he died in 1933.

The educated Greeks of the diaspora of Asia Minor and Egypt were, you said, not only cosmopolitan and, on the whole, well off, they also had a strong and justified sense of a national continuity with the past and felt a direct link that went as far back as at least the Hellenistic period. Their attitude was imperial, not merely ethnic.

You, of the Greek diaspora, were not from a village in the Peloponnesus, nor could you talk of "your island."

There was an Asian cast to your eyes that, as you aged, became more pronounced, so much so you were sometimes taken to be Asian, even by another Greek—this trait from beyond your knowledge of your history, from some Asian in Byzantium, perhaps?

You were always slightly disdainful of Athenian Greeks, as culturally inferior, and kept to yourself, as if to protect all that was left to you after the Catastrophe bereft you of almost everything but your high-minded love of, oh, Bach, of high-minded European culture aspired to by a Constantinopolitan cosmopolitan isolated as a refugee in provincial Athens.

The Greeks of Asia Minor, you said, retained a continuity with their past though defeated by the Ottoman conquest, for they never forgot they were Constantinopolitan.


Stephen called to tell you that W.H. Auden had died, and your voice broke when you tried to speak. You wrote a poem about him, regretting your youthful remark that his craft was mere "polish," as now you saw that his "craft" and he were deeply one, a lesson "too late" for you to learn from him. You used the expression "too late" often. I would ask, "Too late for what?" and you would shrug.

# Zeta

*The griever must rid himself of grief, which he cannot bear, but his will is not strong enough against grief. At moments, he wishes he had never met his lost lover.*

On our first trip together, we went, a summer holiday, to Yugo-slavia, stopping first in Venice. We saw Venice for everything the city contained of Greece: the lions from Delos by the Admiralty, the horses on St. Mark's Basilica from Constantinople, the Byzantine Pala d'Oro coffer behind the main altar, the fresco of a procession headed by one of the Emperor Palaeologus Emperors, and even, it so happened as we passed it, looked in, and entered a service in the Greek Orthodox church.

Walking across St. Mark's Square in Venice, you placed your arm across my shoulders and said that here, within the crowd, we could show our intimacy. I see us, you twenty-nine, I twenty-six, as if from the top of the campanile, walking across the square among the crowd.

In Venice, in a high-ceilinged hotel room with a view of the sea, we, in our large, soft bed with rumpled sheets, made love, the mir-rored doors of the wide armoire open at angles to reflect us. I said, amazed, "Look, look at us!"

At the Venice Biennale, the only pavilion to inspire you was the American, and you said, "Only the Americans are capable of true innovation."

Yugoslavia was a country then united under Communism, and disembarking from the ferry we'd taken from Venice to Opatija, you said about the first Communist country that you entered, "I feel so safe." We visited the Museum of the Revolution, a former fortress on a mountain, with old posters and machine guns, and no one else there. The cicadas shrilled.

In London, we were to meet before the Greek embassy to join a massive demonstration against the dictators. I was early. The curtains of the embassy were drawn. An old woman, wearing tight black clothes, was also waiting. She asked me in Greek if I was Greek, and I responded, no, *Americanos,* and she spit at me. In a rage, I thought of leaving the Greeks to demonstrate their anti-Americanism. But you came along and calmed me: the old woman was most likely an old Communist who was suffering the American-backed dictatorship, or, even earlier, had suffered by the condemnation of Communism in Greece by the Truman Doctrine. You knew more about American foreign policy than I did. We joined the march as it passed the embassy, where, between drawn curtains, someone inside gave the march the finger. In Trafalgar Square, the Greek actress Melina Mercuri, in a tight red blouse, raised her arms and shouted out that Greece would once again inspire freedom in the world, as Greece must do.

We saved enough money to leave Battersea and move back to Marylebone, around the corner from where we had first met, our

address 38 Montagu Square. We kept all the furniture from Battersea, most of it bought at cheap auctions, especially our bed. And so
we established our lives centrally in London, in that world.

During the dictatorship, we spent our summers in Italy, in a small
house in a hamlet called San Andrea di Rovereto, where, night after
night, we made love among coarse sheets; and where, each day, we
walked down a mountain path, past a World War II cement bunker,
to a pebbled beach to swim and, side by side, lie out in sunlight.
And sometimes, our skin as coarse as the sheets with sunlight and
sea salt, returning to our five-shilling house, we went into that dark
bunker, a monument to so much suffering, and there, in narrow
depths, had sex, excited that we should have sex in such a place of
horror, now abandoned.

Stephen Spender visited us secretly in Italy. He took photographs
of us in an olive grove.

You loved Roman Italy, but of course felt, as a Greek, superior,
as Rome too believed Greece superior. And you liked to say that
Greece defeated Italy, commemorated in Greece by the celebration
of the day when Metaxas said, "Οχι!" ("No!") to Mussolini.

You were amused when our Sicilian housekeeper in London,
Maria, called the month of May *maio,* the Sicilian derived from
Greek, instead of *maggio,* the Italian. She was, you liked to say,
from Magna Grecia.

You could claim to be descended from those Romans of Constantine's court, who, though now Greek, still identified their Greekness as Romiosyne, Ρωμιοσύνη.

In Rome, you called yourself ενάς Ρωμιός, a Hellenized Roman, more imperial, sophisticated, and cultured for being Hellenized than a mere Latin Roman.

Your manners were at times imperious, as when you raised your eyes and turned your head away at words you said were beneath your contempt. And from how far back in your imperial history did this gesture date?

We borrowed £3000 from a friend to buy an old stone mill, Il Molino, in Umbria, Italy. You drew a plan: the orchard, the pond for ducks, the outbuilding for a cow. We helped the farmers (not peasants, but *coltivatori diretti*) with the *vendemmia* for making wine, with the harvesting of wheat, with the threshing. We were going to live there, make our wine, grow our vegetables, preserve fruit and berries for the winter. A friend called us Bouvard and Pécuchet, after the absurdly idealistic couple in Flaubert's book of the same name.

In a small Italian town on our way to Il Molino, where we stopped to spend the night, there was a festival put on by *l'Unita*, the Communist newspaper, with red flags hanging from branches of trees and long tables of food. An old woman asked us to join in singing "The Internationale," which you did in Greek. I did not know the

Communist anthem. You liked being in a country where the Communist flag could be shown.

We didn't go to Greece until seven years passed and the dictatorship was overthrown there. We drove from our home in London to Hastings, by ferry across the Channel to Calais and down through France, spending nights in provincial French towns, then across the Alps into Italy and Il Molino. And then from Il Molino through Umbria and the Marches to Ancona, then by ferry to Eugemenitsa in Epirus, and from there down to Athens. England, France, Italy, Greece, these were united in our languages, and in our love, too, for United Europe. Though I retained my American citizenship, I had become a British citizen to belong with you to the European Union.

Driving through the mountains of Epirus, hot and thirsty, we got out at a roadside fountain, a stream of water jetting from a hole in what might have been a marble stele for the dead—but surrounded by litter we collected, heaped together, and burned—then, stripped naked, we washed and drank the cold, clear, sweet water.

When I read in *The Greek Anthology* of a fountain of cool water under a breeze-shaken elm, where the weary stranger may drink and rest from the intense heat, I think of us both at the fountain in the mountains of Epirus.

You introduced me to *The Greek Anthology*—a compilation of epigrams first put together as a garland by Meleager, sometime between 100 and 90 BC, which garland was incorporated into a greater garland in 40 AD by Philip of Thessolonika, which garland was incorporated into the anthology of Kephalas in the fourth century, which anthology was included in the anthology of the Byzantine Maximus Planudes, circa 1255–1305, which was printed in 1484, a selection from this you gave to me as a gift published in 1971—and I read and reread these short stark poems as the expression of grief that grief demands: simple, clear, timeless.

I try to translate:
*Mindlessly as you go on your way,*
*When you see Thrason's tomb, stranger, stop and have pity.*

When we, at Dodona, stood under a holm oak, a descendant of a tree from which the temple priests hung tiny silver cymbals to interpret the sounds they made as winds, soft or hard, blew through the branches, I thought that such Greek oracles had meaning for us both and, retrospectively, presaged our love.

We visited Thermopylae, where a ruined stone wall seemed to be made of black ash, and there I imagined the Spartan soldiers combing and coiffing their long hair, which the Persians, from their distance, understood meant that the Spartans were preparing to die. The Persians won, and, centuries later, the Germans won at Thermopylae.

By the time we arrived in Greece, in Athena's city of bare, red earth and broken orange trees along the marble curbs, we had already founded our own country in our love with its own history, the history of two lovers tessellated in blue and gold mosaic. I hated Greece that first time.

I wanted Greece to be as beautiful as I fantasized the country to be before I went, and was shocked by the brutal use of tractors, cement building blocks, poured cement. I complained to you about this brutality, and you said, "But Greece is not your fantasy."

You told me that, if I were to fulfill my fantasy of being in Pericles' Athens, I would be shocked by the smell of shit, the garbage and scavenging dogs in the narrow streets, the derelict houses.

Your mother appeared to me of Constantinopolitan refinement, whose most expressive gesture of her love for you was to tap you lightly on your arm and smile delicately, delicately sad.

Your unmarried aunt, you said, still had her dowry, hidden in a caddy of chamomile tea.

When something went missing, your aunt immediately accused the maid, which enraged you. But she reminded you of the red-bound collection of Shakespeare's plays, from which the gold initials of your father, once tacked to the covers, had been stolen by a maid.

(But when, in London, something went missing in our apartment, you immediately accused Maria, and I became enraged.)

There seemed to me little that was Greek in your mother's apartment: on a shelf in a bookcase a tiny icon, so black with soot the image was invisible, a fragment of plaster molding from a neoclassical house, two small carved chairs from an island, and that's all.

The rugs and silver were from Turkey, taken from Constantinople.

I noted, on a corner of the desk in the study, a glass jar painted with naked youths by Tsarouchis, in which pencils were kept. You brought this back to London, as if transferring your Greek life to our London life. And you brought back many of your books on philosophy.

Among the books in the study were those you had had while studying in America, and I was brought back to my own past from before I met you, seeing books I too had read: the poetry of Walt Whitman, of Ezra Pound, of Wallace Stevens. Stevens was a great influence on your own poetry, and you sometimes used lines directly from his to claim a new vision of reality.

I noted an old 78 rpm record player, in an elegant 1930s case, and you played to me the heavy, black records you used to listen to when young: Schnabel playing Bach.

We went to visit the tomb of your father, which you washed. Nearby, a group of mourners at a tomb gathered, you said, for *minimosima,* the day of remembrance forty days after the death of the beloved. One came and offered us *koliva,* a mixture of boiled wheat, raisins, parsley, sugar, and cinnamon, sometimes with almonds and pomegranate seeds, passed about among other visitors to the cemetery in little white paper bags with black crosses on them. You said *koliva* came from ancient times.

In Athens, our historical differences were demonstrated to me simply when you showed me a diploma of your mother's from Roberts College in Constantinople on papyrus, diplomas being for me on sheepskin.

Taking me about the city, in the Athenian Agora you made me aware of the different layers of history in the Archaic, Classical, Hellenistic, Roman, Byzantine, and Ottoman fragments.

In this city of many layers of history, you showed me all the places that had been central to your youth: the apartment block behind the cathedral where you lived with your aunt in a *retiré,* from the balcony on which you had watched the flares illuminate the far airport and bombs fall, in agony about the cat you had had to leave behind.

We looked into the entrance hall of the apartment block, and you said you often dreamed of the white-and-black-patterned marble floor.

You brought me into the cathedral, where you taught me how to kiss the icons—pressing the tip of the nose to the glass and kissing the air. We lit candles, thin, browning, beeswax candles, which were then stuck in sand in a brass stand.

We went to neoclassical Athens College, which your father designed, and you showed me the wing where you had boarded for eight years.

You wanted me to see the house in Elleniko, now rented out, where you had lived your young years, before your father died. The sagging bougainvillea covered the entire facade.

We walked through the large garden, overgrown, the fruit trees unattended, to the wall beyond which had been the German canteen, now a ruin, bombed by the British.

We passed a derelict building at the edge of a weed-grown lot, which, you told me, was where people opposed to the dictatorship were brought and tortured. You asked, how could that building ever be purified?

In Athens, you suffered terrible migraines, as if Athena herself caused them. Together in the bedroom we shared, you would press your forehead against my chest.

The time we climbed up to the Acropolis, visitors were allowed to walk among the pillars of the Parthenon in moonlight, which we both did, and there you kissed me, as if all your life in Athens you had wanted to do that.

Not long after the death of W.H. Auden, we saw in Athens his lover, Chester Kalman, a grotesque man who sat all afternoon in a *kafenio* drinking ouzo, surrounded at the small table by the boys he bought. You said they protected him, and commiserated when he, weeping, grieved the death of Yannis, the boy he loved, who allowed him so much life—Τόσο πολλή ζωή.

With one red rose, you went alone to visit the poet Yannis Ritsos, who had been interned in a camp on an isolated, stark island during the dictatorship for being a Communist. You translated his poems. In one, a young and handsome man stands against a wall, his eyes uncovered, waiting to be shot, and he feels calm. Years later when Communism fell, you said the poet, defeated, took to his bed and died.

On an excursion to the island of Poros, you told me that you had last been there years ago with a lover who had abandoned you, and, alone, you'd sat on rocks, the air filled with the essence of the scent of lemon blossoms from across the sea, your consolation.

Now that you were able to return to Greece, you said you missed the Greek sun and sea.

Still, Italy—*Italia! Italia!* as Aeneas hears Italy call to him—held us with the belief that we would live at Il Molino. But after years of arriving to find the roof leaked, the pump did not work to bring water from the well, the fields were high with weeds, you regretfully agreed the house must be sold. I was struck by this: your vital attachment to places, and your sense of defeat when having to give them up, as if you were fated to give up places that centered your life. We sold Il Molino for £30,000, more money than we had ever had separately.

You said I was the more willful one, and I, the more willful one, became determined that you must have both Greece *and* Italy. You knew little about the Greek islands, but an English hippie advised: go to the island of Paros, go to the other side of the island from the port to the village of Marpissa, and there a house will be found. We went, and found a derelict house in the village for £6,000, with a large, marble-floored main room, front and back courtyards, and a roof terrace with a view across the Aegean to Naxos.

And Italy? Alone, I went to Lucca, where we'd been and where we'd felt encircled by the town's old walls, and for £10,000 I bought an apartment at the top of a thirteenth-century tenement building, Corte Pini, near the medieval Tower of the Hours. I had all our rustic furniture from Il Molino moved to Corte Pini and waited for your arrival from London. You told me I was the willful one, but you were the critical one, and I was apprehensive that you wouldn't like the apartment. Without taking off your overcoat—it was winter— you examined the rooms, looked out of the windows over roofs to the distant Appenine Mountains, said nothing. More apprehensive, I said, "You don't like the place," and you, frowning deeply, said, "Why do you always presume to know what I think and feel?" I bit my lower lip, sure that you would be critical. You said, "I love it."

We went to Lucca for winter holidays. New Year's Eve, our habit at midnight was to walk on the walls, the mist so dense the light from the fireworks set off from the battlements were diffused in the mist. Then home, and a fire in the wood-burning stove, and a bottle of *prosecco,* and a game of Scrabble, which you always won. And I would think: oh, that my Love be content, be happy! You were not really content, not really happy, except, perhaps, at moments, at such moments.

One New Year's Eve, I insisted we go into the center of the town to the Piazza del Anfiteatro, built on the ancient Roman Coliseum, packed with people who were drinking from foaming bottles and throwing firecrackers among feet. You, angry, insisted on leaving, and I thought: you never take pleasure in anything, are even resentful of my taking pleasure. I became angry. We had an argument and were silent on our way home, where, without a fire, *prosecco,* or Scrabble, we prepared for bed. In bed, you said, "You don't understand. I'm frightened of crowds, terrified of explosions."

On Paros, during our summer holidays there, you set the routine, each day the same, the walk down to the sea with a lunch of two tomatoes, swimming and sunbathing on our little beach just big enough for us to lie on, the walk home as the sun declined, the meal of lentils in the courtyard, and *ousakia* on the terrace as the sun declined and the streetlights came on in the village and we watched the full moon rise red over Naxos, rise huge and, rising, concentrate itself into an intense white globe that shone along the sea to us, shone on the bottle of ouzo, the carafe of water, the glasses, the seashell on the marble tabletop, and shone on us, making us and all about us ghostly. Then to bed. The days to you were not repeated, you said, but were of infinite variations.

But even here, in the main square of the island village of Marpissa, was a bright white marble statue of a youth, naked to the waist, his hands tied behind his back, who, on a sweet morning of June, was hanged by the Nazi occupier. His name was Nicolas Stella.

In Marpissa, when there was a wedding there were also fireworks. You would go out into the narrow streets and shout to have the fireworks stopped—they frightened the birds. And seeing cartridges left in the countryside by hunters, you said you wished birds had rifles to shoot back.

In homage to the brightness of the Greek sun, you quoted from I did not know where:

Ἡλίου τε φώς[1]

and when I asked, you said you couldn't remember the source, your references deeper than your own memory, deep in the memory of your history.

You taught me expressions from ancient Greek, such as, each morning on waking:

ῥοδοδάκτυλοσ Ἡώς[2]

---

1. O light of the sun
2. Rosy-fingered dawn

or, as we approached the sea on our daily walk:

θαλλασά! θαλλασά!³

From our little beach, you swam out far, so far I sometimes couldn't see the splash your swimming made, and, standing to search the Aegean Sea waves, asked myself, alarmed: What if he drowned? What if he died?

We aged. On a ferry to Paros, you plucked a gray hair from my head and threw it into the dark Aegean Sea.

At Delphi with you, in falling snow, I imagined asking the Sybille, "Σίβιλλα τί θέλεις;" ("What do you want, Sybille?"), and, answering for her, "ἀποθανειν θέλω" ("I want to die"). But you corrected me: "Ζήν θέλω!" ("I want to live!")

---

3. The sea! The sea!

# Eta

Our Gods were different. Your Eastern God loved the temporal world, loved incense and chant and gold vestments, loved flowers, these offerings meant to please Him. But to my Western God I prayed, beyond the temporal, to be with Him in eternity, which was His pleasure.

Your Greek God, closed behind the iconostasis, was unknowable and beyond reasonable proof of His existence, apophatic. My God, Roman, could be approached openly through reason, with ten proofs of His existence declared by St. Thomas in his Summa Theologica. The Orthodox Church did not have an Aquinas, but the hymns of St. John of Damascus. As I was attracted to your God, so were you attracted to mine, as I longed for the unknowable and you for the knowable. Yet, meeting as we did in what we both longed for in each other, we were also drawn back to what our Gods longed for in us—that, His being beyond reason, you should not question, and that, His being within reason, I should.

During Holy Week in Athens, day after day we went to a church service in Plaka, following on Good Friday the Epitaphios, Christ embroidered in silver and in gold on a silk shroud laden with rose petals and wet with scent sprayed from vials, and carried by boys three times around the small church as a nun tolled a bell hung from a branch of a tree (all that day, all over Athens, bells tolled). After the burial and the resurrection at midnight between Saturday and Easter Sunday, when we left with the dispersing crowd, holding, as all did, lit candles to mark with soot-rising flame the lintel of the doorway of home, I asked you, "Do you believe in God?" and you answered, "That's a question I never ask myself."

Opinions you always saw as personal and irrelevant to what you believed great, for impersonal greatness existed for you and need not be questioned. You once said, "There is no question that Bach believed in God."

No mystic, you, more Aristotelian than Platonic, and I more Platonic than Aristotelian—though, given you were Eastern and I Western, I would have expected the opposite to be true of us. Your impulse was to point downward, to find in the world love absolute, to find it in your love for me; and mine to point upward, beyond the world, and perhaps beyond you. You believed love rose from the body ("I love your body"); I, a debased Plotinus, believed love was disembodied ("I love your soul").

How confused I become thinking of you and me as one, wondering how much of you I have made mine, how much of me I have made yours—combining in us both mind and soul, as if these two were one, and Aristotle and Plato, too.

Perhaps because reason so dominated your thinking, and your feeling, too, you were drawn to Greek surrealism, a mode of poetry with deep roots in Greek peasant songs, as irrational as "clouds of sheep," or "the moon-street on the sea," or "it's raining chair legs."

You liked a Greek folk poem, which you said originated in the deep tradition of native Greek surrealism, and in which kisses turn lips red, and when the lips are wiped on a handkerchief the handkerchief turns red, and the handkerchief when washed in a river turns the river red, and the river running into the sea turns the sea red, and an eagle drinking red water becomes red, and the sun and the moon become red.

If you ever thought of me as an idealist and you as a realist, you were right, even though you did sustain ideals—insisting that they be aspired to temporally, in politics, in culture, in love, in your poetry, and even in religion. And I, the true idealist, believed ideals were realized only in eternity. I could pledge you love forever, whereas you could pledge me love at 4:15 P.M. next Tuesday— a true sign, according to W. H. Auden, of love.

You told me to convert to Greek Orthodoxy.

You started a lecture on "Some Sources of Modern Greek Poetry" with a recording of a fifth-century Greek Byzantine Friday Lenten Service of the Akathistos Hymn, Salutations to the Virgin:

*Awed by the beauty of your purity . . .*

In your purity, you were able to use words I, impure, could not—you as pure as the young man, the Archon of Plateae, who wore white and for a year did not touch iron, the culmination of the procession to the heroes' tombs where he poured out libations and prayed.

You used the word "purity," but would you have tried to define the idea of purity? No, and certainly not as dogma, which you saw as tyrannical. You used the word this way: he is pure, animals are pure, the scent of lemon blossoms is pure, the taste of lemon is pure, the sunlight is pure, music is pure, and kisses, too, are pure. And this, the most undefined preposition: love at love's brightest is pure.

All throughout your poetry, you used such words that I found foreign, you a Greek, I now an Anglo-American. You used the word "antinomy," in Greek αντινομία, and in your poems worked to bring together all "oppositions of one law to another," all "contradictions between conclusions which seem equally logical, reasonable, or necessary," and resolve them in the purity of your poetry.

The antinomies in you were from deep in your history: your belief in Classical freedom and your need for Byzantine order.

Parmenides believed that reality is one, Heraclitus that reality is infinitely many; Parmenides believed that nothing can come to be or pass away, and Heraclitus that everything comes to be and passes away.

In your thesis, for your MA at Denison University, you wrote about Emmanuel Kant: "In his philosophy, the aesthetic dimension—beauty—occupies the central position between sensuousness and morality—the two poles of human existence."

In the same thesis, you quoted Nietzsche: "Beauty is therefore, for the artists, something outside of all order or rank, because in beauty antitheses are bound together."

Nietzsche's books, you argued, all together "cohered," not "logically" as philosophy, but "formally" as in a work of art, the "form" containing "an infinite number of inconsistencies." Nietzsche's "form" was cyclical, was repetition revolving on repetition, each repetition an elaboration.

In the slow evolution of Greek, back further than Homeric Greek, ιδέα meant not "idea" so much as "form," so, back then, "the idea of the body" was "the form of the body." And so, to "reason" for you was to reason in "forms."

Pindar describes a beautiful athlete "ιδέα τε καλόν," rendered into English "beautiful of form," making idea form, good beautiful.

You wrote in a poem, "I love your body," as if love was for you embodied in the senses, and yet more than the senses together, an enveloping sense itself sensuous, as if all the body made sense.

Though you published two books of poems in Greece—books that were not noted because, you said, you would not play the Greek game of ingratiating yourself with the critics—you did not even try to publish in England. But you were asked from time to time to give readings, which a friend, the art historian and artist John Golding, attended, writing later in your obituary in the *Times*: "What Nikos sought from poetry throughout his life was formal invention, not simply for its own sake, but at the service of delving into new ways of perceiving reality and conveying depth of feeling." And: "His own poetry has about it a lyric plangency, as if he was trying to recapture scenes, states of mind, relationships, all glimpsed but never fully seized." I would say: never fully revealed, for what most conceals in your poetry is the plangency, which seems to draw the reader to see through the plangency to the sensitive intelligence behind, but which entrances in itself. And so the tension in your poetry, the antinomies of the concealed and the revealed, the mysterious concealed and the to-be-revealed essential purity of your thought and feeling, the tension resolved in, as you wrote, in the pure light of ultimate knowledge.

Philosophy was so much a part of your poetry you could use philosophical terms and give them poetic sense—"sense" more than "meaning"—meaning that you imbued the term with such pure brightness it became its brightness more than it remained a term—and in the purity of that brightness you did resolve the antinomy of thought and feeling, making in your poetry all thought feeling, all feeling thought—and to you the brightest "categorical imperative," the ultimate resolution of body with mind, mind with body, was "love," that most philosophical of terms.

Your longest poem, on which you worked over years, is "Pure Reason," a reflection on all the changes in our love over the years in which you must find the essence of love: an inward necessity, clear and simple in itself, a categorical imperative.

How sad so many of your poems are, my Love, how sad, the full expression of your "defeat," your "ruin":
*They have lost their faith.*

*And so the unaccomplished will remain unaccomplished.*

*Uncertainty will be their neutral light.*

And how filled with longing:
*I want my landscape to be seen in the sharp light,*
*The ultimate clarification, the essential metaphor,*
*the "essential" and the "central" poem.*

And:
*You* have *to believe.*

And:
*Soon you will learn the 'meaning' you have been so embarrassingly*
*and childishly craving for.*

My reassurance—so much a need now—is to read your love for me in your poems:

*Your body flutters sometimes when we sleep.*
*I try to hold you.*
*That is when I think that perhaps you*
*Know the secret of the weather.*

When you exclaimed, "Oh the marvelous!" I sensed a sphere clearly defined by its own light and turning round and round, emitting light and music.

Idly reading an anthology of Greek literature, Greek on one page and on the facing page English, I try to fit the Greek into the English, and think of you as when I read, in the *Phaedo* of Plato, Socrates, imprisoned and about to die, affirming in English that "philosophy was the greatest kind of music," and in Greek φιλοσοφίας μέν ούσης μεγίστης μουσικής.

# Theta

We were separated for periods, as when I taught at the University of East Anglia, but I returned to London every weekend. One weekend, I arrived to find you had prepared an elaborate meal, an Anatolian dish I liked called *kidonato*—lamb with quince. During the meal, you were deeply, stiffly silent. I asked why. "Nothing," you said. But I kept on: Why? You had called me in the cottage where I lived on the campus and someone, clearly a young man, had answered, not I. "That was a student I allowed to study in my sitting room when I wasn't there," I said. You looked at me doubtfully. "Honestly," I said. You relaxed. I remained amazed: that you should have prepared such a meal for me, believing that I'd been unfaithful to you.

Our longest periods of separation were when I became a professor at Columbia University in New York and was away from you half the year, for the spring and autumn semesters. My constant longing was to return to you, and when I did, taking a night flight after my last class that got me into London at dawn, I would find the door to our flat in Montagu Square locked from the inside. I had to ring the bell and wake you. Opening the door, you appeared a little resentful, as if I had disturbed my absence.

I saw that you were able now to write your poetry only in my absence, and many poems about my absence, which became a presence to you.

Away from you in New York, I bought a gold chain to give to you, bought it with someone I had loved before I met you but who had not loved me, Öçi. I had met him as a student in Spain and he now lived in New York, where he took me to the Hasidic jewelry shops on West 47th Street. You lost the chain—a link broke and it fell from your neck; you had no idea where. Telling me, your regret was, "You bought it for me with Öçi!" who, since I had bought the chain with him, had died.

You came to New York on publishing business and stayed with me in what I thought of as our apartment there. On each visit, you bought another piece of furniture, and I loved this, your assuming my place away from you was also your place. You arranged the furniture, which I kept as you had arranged it after you left. Our idea was that after you retired from publishing, we would live together in New York while I taught at Columbia, adding to our other worlds the revolving world of New York. Once when you were with me in New York, a snowstorm closed the airports, and I wished they would stay closed forever so you would not be able to leave.

On every subsequent return to our home in London, I felt that you yourself were more absent, and I worried about you. We no longer made love, the expression of our love to press our foreheads together and stare into each other's eyes. You hardly smiled.

I knew, deeply, that you did not want to talk about your state, as you never would talk about any "problem" between us, but, daring to, I waited until we were in Lucca, as usual for our winter holiday, to ask you what was wrong. We were walking on the walls, the sky as bright as ice. You said, "Nothing is wrong," and I wondered if you said this to reassure me, or if you yourself believed nothing was wrong. You did not know any more than I did that you were ill.

I noted how thin you were, your face as refined in its features as a Byzantine mosaic.

Low in spirits, you became spirited when the niece of Steven Runciman called you in London and you went to see her in her club, returning with the bronze cockerel he had promised you would inherit.

When I was with you and you appeared to become more and more absent, my need to glorify you became greater and greater. How to glorify you? Glorify you most in this: as lover?

I, who so often envied the world, thought: Let the world envy me for the love I have in you!

No one else, ever, had a lover who loved as you did me.

I asked, Why did you love me? and then asserted, as if no question was raised, *You loved me!* and was amazed.

I remembered the elderly woman who had once told me that I would love you more as we grew older together.

In New York, I called you every day. You worried about your cats, who were not well.

Our closest friend, Julia, told me, when I called her from New York, that she had almost stopped trying to get you out to a recital, to a play, to an exhibition. You had become reclusive.

Did I sometimes think: has his love gone?

I arrived in London, the dawn as dark as night, and rang the bell to wake you and have you come open the door. You looked thinner, your face now contorted with gauntness, and you scowled. I reached out to hold you, but you drew back. In our bedroom, as I changed from the clothes I'd worn traveling into pajamas and a bathrobe, you began to shout: Your life was a failure, you were in despair, you wanted to die. Again, I reached out to hold you, but again you drew away, scowling. I lay on our bed, wanting you to lie next to me, simply lie next to me. You went out of the room. I lay shivering. After an hour, you came back into the room and lay down beside me and, as when we first met, you put an arm about me as to comfort me.

How, now, could *I* cure *you?* I did not know what your illness was and thought the history you had endured had finally defeated you. And how could I cure you of *that?*

You said that you were not frightened of death, even said, "Death is a part of life," which I did not understand, and only now try to.

I was with you for a week, during which I watched over you carefully, not wanting you to be disturbed. And, oh yes, we slept together nights through, long nights. And then I must return to New York.

Our doctor in London called me in New York to say I must come back to you; you were very ill with "horrendous" cancer. I did, within one day, and when you opened the door to me, I, my arms open, wept. You stepped back, and holding out your hands to keep me back, insisted, "No, no," and I resolved: I must be practical.

I didn't want you to know you were dying, but our doctor said you knew. If you knew, you showed no fear, as if your belief that death is a part of life would carry you through. You worried, simply, what would happen to your cats.

My instances of anger towards you when, though I knew you were dying, you raged against me for a dirty dish I left in the kitchen sink—I should have been more patient, should have understood that, as you sensed the ultimate disorder of your life, you needed order more than ever.

As you became ill, you became more effusive in expressions of love when speaking to friends than to me, giving them "masses" of your love, giving "all" your love, giving your love "ever." You did not say this to me.

I went with you every time you had an appointment at the clinic for chemotherapy, you in a large cushioned chair, a tube by a needle inserted in a vein attaching you to a plastic bag of chemicals suspended from a pole, while I got coffee for you or a newspaper or simply sat beside you, you finding it all funny, as if you went along with it, quite sure it wouldn't help, with a light spirit.

I think you separated yourself from yourself dying, and looked on that self with some humor.

We sat together, alone in the clinic's waiting room, for your appointment with the oncologist. When called, you rose with difficulty, but smiling, as if amused, and walked unsteadily away. The receptionist, a black woman at a desk in a corner of the waiting room, came to sit beside me when she saw me weep, and said, "You've got to be strong for both of you." I remember you walking away from me.

I watched you, ill, wander all about the room to try to find a drawer to fit in it the plate of lentils I'd prepared. I thought: this isn't strange, no, nothing's strange, no.

You began to see cats—white cats—flying through the air, and this vision made you laugh.

You knew you had tumors, spinal, lung, brain, but you saw no causal relationship between these and your memory loss and confusion, or even your becoming weaker day by day, causality now for you merely an illusion.

You needed a walking stick. I wanted you to have a silver-topped one, but you insisted on one cheap. I thought, then, he'll recover and won't need a stick, so the cheap one will do for now.

At moments away from you, out shopping while our house-keeper, Maria, looked after you, I asked myself: Did I want you to die, as though your death were a strange fulfillment of my love for you? I'd stop, stand still in the street, overwhelmed by this: the sense, a sensation throughout my body and, too, my soul, that you must live.

I sometimes asked myself in the pages of my diary (wanting in those pages to account for every thought, every feeling) if your death would liberate me from our lives together to live an altogether other life with radiating possibilities. My answer to myself, as near as I could get to a central truth, was no—I wanted, at that center, no other life, but my life radiating in you.

I cannot read my diaries from the time of your illness to your death and after, frightened of the revelations in them of thoughts and feelings I'd rather forget.

As your mind went, not knowing where you were, or, perhaps, who you were, you poured cologne onto your nightshirt as if to give body to yourself in the beautiful scent.

You lay on the rug of the sitting room floor to listen to Bach partitas, the only music you could listen to, recorded by Richard Goode. You'd sometimes sit up and exclaim, as if amazed, "I know every note!"

Entering the bathroom, I saw you standing before the washbasin, after chemotherapy, brushing your hair out in falling clumps. I was alarmed, but you said matter-of-factly, "My hair will grow back." I said I would clear up, and did, to save a lock.

Together, we made and remade our bed to satisfy your need for order—to the detail that the label on the blanket had to be on the lower-left corner of the bed—but the bed was never made right.

Again and again, you asked, "Why aren't I better?"

A friend wrote, "Fate is cruel, trafficking in nightmares." I asked myself why I did not feel this applied to you, but was too general to apply to you, to anyone in particular.

I did not feel that religious faith applied to you, to us. Religion applied to others, but not to you, for faith was too general, and you in dying were too particular for such generalizations.

I woke you from a nap to tell you I was going out to shop for supper. When I returned, you were up, walking about in your pajamas, agitated. Alarmed, you asked, "Where were you? I was so worried."

You had forgotten I'd told you I'd be out. I helped you back into bed, then lay beside you. You took one of my hands in your thin, cold hand and brought it to your chest. "Thank God you came back," you said.

Every night, in bed with you, I thought: I am falling asleep with someone who is dying. All during the night, often woken by you because your back pained you, I'd think: I'm in bed with someone who is dying.

Most of the days, during the intervals from sleep when you were half asleep, you would ask me, over and over, what day it was, where your cats were, what was happening. I asked you, "Are you anxious?" You asked, "About what?" I didn't want to say, about dying, because I didn't want you to know, but wondered if you did. Puzzled by my question, you answered, "No."

You became frustrated when you couldn't remember what you were just about to say, something that, clearly, remained as a *sense* for which you had forgotten the words. Frowning, staring out as you tried to concentrate, you looked haunted.

One evening, you looked at me then turned away and asked, "Where is David?" Shocked, I wondered: does he mean some other David? You turned back to me and said, "You, you're David."

Together in our bed, falling asleep, you said, "I can't tell where the edges of the bed are."

Asleep in our bed one early morning, I was awakened by you calling from the bathroom. You were sitting naked on the toilet, your pajamas in a heap on the floor. You were whimpering. Your thighs were covered in shit. Naked myself from bed, I cleaned you, then drew a bath and helped you into it, and you shat more in the water. I helped you out, sat you on the edge of the tub, from where you shat into the tub. I wiped your anus and buttocks, washed you, unplugged the tub to let the water and shit drain out, wrapped you, shivering, in a towel, washed out the tub, filled it again with hot soapy water, hefted you back into the tub and washed you thoroughly. You gave in to me, helplessly, as I hefted you from the tub, dried you, dressed you in clean pajamas, and, trembling as you were, supported you back into bed. Exhausted, naked still, I lay next to you and we both fell asleep.

In our bed, you twisted and turned, exclaiming that no one told you what was going on, no one told you anything, everyone kept secrets from you. You didn't know where you were or what was happening. I tried to calm you by lying beside you, but you were too agitated, and, facing me, you said, "I know I take up all your time, but still you don't have time to help me," and at this, facing you, I wept. Unmoved by my tears, you continued to criticize me, irrationally, for not helping you. I swear: I wept, not for myself, but for you. I wondered if I should leave you alone, as that seemed to be what you wanted, but decided no, I must remain with you, lying beside you, and, without comment, listen. You didn't become calm, but in your confusion interrogated me about who was ringing the bell of the street door, though no one was ringing. You suspected conspiracy against you, in which I played a part.

In my study, off the landing from our bedroom, I would suddenly become aware of the deep, deep silence from our bedroom, where you, asleep, were as if already dead.

Sometimes, unsteadily, you would come down to the sitting room where I was to lie on the sofa and doze, and I, in an armchair reading a novel, would sense the deepest comfort, you lying still and calm.

Why, I asked myself, was your total dependence on me reassuring to me? Why did your total dependency on me liberate me of all other thoughts and feelings I had had about you, purifying me? I didn't understand.

You struggled against my bathing you—the bathroom was too cold, I wasn't supporting you securely enough, you would slip and fall, the water was too hot—but after, when you were back in our bed, you said, "You do too much for me." And I, "I do because I love you," and I kissed your forehead. You smiled—a smile I hadn't seen in a very long while—and you said, "And I love you." I wondered if you knew what this meant.

You had not been out of our home for weeks except to go to the clinic for treatment. You asked, "Did we go to that reception two days ago?" You made a face of disdain. "All these dinner parties, all this socializing."

When I went into our bedroom and saw you, eyes staring out, I asked you what you were seeing. You said, "I see clouds moving on the ceiling," and then, "No, just cracks."

As I watched you in the bath, like a boy washing yourself, washing carefully your cock, drawing the foreskin back to reveal your delicate glans, I thought of all those Saturday afternoons when we made love, then fell asleep together.

Our doctor, who came regularly, told me I must go out, must see friends. But I didn't want to go out, didn't want to see anyone but you. I wanted to become closer to you, and if I were to go out I wanted to go far, to take you away with me.

You said, clearly, "Obviously my mind is not working," and with this I thought you *can* be rational, you *can* have insights, but immediately you began to complain that no one, no one, including me, had told you what was wrong with you. I said, "I don't know," and this was true: I didn't and don't know anything about death.

Sometimes you amused me. Not able to put on a bathrobe, holding it upside down and trying to find the sleeves, you said, exasperated, "This country—nothing is right in this country."

As always hoping that my presence reassured you, I lay beside you. You were awake. Reverting to the childish talk we in the past sometimes indulged in, I asked you, "Do you love me?" You said, "I do." I asked, "How much?" You held up your hands to indicate a

space and said, "That much. Is it enough?" And I said, "It's enough."
You smiled, so rare now, indulging me, I for this moment the child
you, the adult, must reassure.

Calmly, you said, "I wish I could go home."
"But we are at home. You don't think we are?"
"Not quite."
"Where is home, then?"
"In London," you said, and then, "This is London."
"It is, and we're at home here."
"Not quite," you said again.
"Is Greece home?"
"No, not quite." You were silent, trying to think, then you said,
"Home has many meanings."

One morning, waking, you said, "I don't want to despair." As
clear as your voice was, I wondered if you knew the meaning of
your words, as I knew less and less the meanings of the words as
you uttered them.

As weak as you were, you wanted to show me you were *not* dependent on me, and, dressing yourself as you insisted, you went
down to the kitchen, I following, to wash two glasses left in the sink,
to wash them furiously in clouds of suds, the fury against me for not
helping, but causing your agitation and confusion.

You shouted at me, "I know what you want. You don't want me to
be better. You want me to be worse. You want me to die."

You fell onto our bed, barely able to move, so I had to arrange you and cover you. I lay next to you, watching you, your eyes slowly closing then opening again and again, so many expressions passing across your face, at moments your eyebrows raised in wonder, at others your brow in a frown, at others you smiled a little.

I spent most days lying beside you on our bed. As the room darkened with the sunset, you began to talk to yourself in whispers. I didn't know if you were asleep or awake, but knew you were awake when you asked to hold me. You put an arm across my chest and began to feel, delicately, all my chest, then you plucked at the tee shirt I was wearing. Again, I wasn't sure if you were asleep or awake, but from your breathing thought you must be asleep. You now pulled at the cloth of my tee shirt as I lay still, wondering what, what was going on in your mind. Suddenly you stopped pulling and said, quietly, "It's gone."

You said, "I walked in the red forest."

As you drifted in and out of sleep, you asked questions: "Where are my keys?" "How much was that bottle of wine?" "Did you see the Nazi invasion?"

You, in bed, reached out a hand to me and asked, "Will you take this?" I rose from my chair by the bed to hold out my hand and you handed me nothing, which I took.

Asleep or not, your eyes open, you said, "When we were very poor . . . " Then, it seemed with total self-awareness, you suddenly said, "I'm just saying out loud what I'm dreaming."

You said, "Something very funny happened in Athens. It was Christmas, the church bells were ringing, firecrackers were exploding—" You laughed. "She was mesmerized." You laughed again, and I laughed with you.

You often examined your hands, and once took one of my hands to examine closely, but then, as if you'd seen what you wanted to see, or perhaps seen what you hadn't wanted to see, you threw my hand away from you.

You spoke in whispers to yourself, but all at once addressed me. "What's the same?" I said, "You tell me." You said, "Μπρός και εμπρός.[4] They're the same." You were very pleased with yourself. "You see, I found it."

My wonder at your state of mind was sometimes "scientific," as when, seeing you hold out your hands to study them, you said, "I can't see any depth." I asked, "Can you see your hands?" "I can," you answered, "but they're not my hands."

---

4. The two Greek words Μπρός and εμπρός are synonyms; both mean "forward, ahead, in front."

We slept some, and I woke to you searching my chest with your fingers. You laid your hand on my chest and for a while were still. I wondered what, what I meant to you—not as myself, not as someone who lived with you, but as someone or something larger than I was, someone or something I embodied but wasn't.

You clasped my hand and brought it close to your mouth and moved your lips as though to kiss it or to drink from my palm, and I suddenly sobbed. Immediately, violently, you threw my hand away and shouted, "Stop it!" I did. For a long while after you wouldn't let me hold your hand, but pushed mine away when I reached out for yours, and said again and again, "Φύγε, φύγε, φύγε."[5]

You were grimacing, a horror, I thought, occurring to you in a dream. I leaned over you and whispered, "Είμαι η αγάπη σου,"[6] and, oh, I saw your face become calm.

Naked, washed by a night nurse, you appeared to me ready to be embalmed and mummified, your encaustic portrait, garlanded, to be inserted above your mummified face, a Greek in Egypt, to be buried in Fayyum.

My Love, naked as when we made love.

---

5. Go away, go away, go away.
6. I'm your love.

A strange sense came over me—not of elation, though something like elation, but not any other sense I could explain. I felt I was outside myself, and that you, too, were outside yourself.

I asked, again, "Do you know who I am?" You took a long time to say, "You're David." I asked, "What's your name?" Your brow furrowed with your thinking, and you turned your face away. You couldn't remember your name. I said, "Nikos Stangos," and you began to weep, to weep, I thought, because you couldn't remember your name. I asked, "Do you know where we live?" Not answering, you looked at me. I said, "38 Montagu Square." You wept more, wept and sobbed, and I wiped your tears away with tissue after tissue. I said, in Greek, "It's our home, 38 Montagu Square." Sobbing, you said in Greek, "Let's sleep." I lowered my forehead to yours and, oh God, my tears dripped into your tears.

Then this: when I drew back a little, my face close to yours, you raised your thin, delicate hands to the sides of my face and tenderly touched me.

There's vanity in proclaiming: I accepted, stoically, my Lover's suffering, fed him, bathed him, lay beside him to comfort him, as if all that I endured, he didn't.

I began to put order in our home, and decided to throw out objects that were meaningful to you before you died, such as an old amaryllis reduced to one limp leaf that you had insisted on nurturing because it was still alive. I must throw out such objects you were attached to, as I knew that after you died, I wouldn't be able to.

I sat at your desk in your study to put order in the long, last poem you were working on: *TI ΕΣΤΙΝ ΑΛΗΘΕΙΑ;* (WHAT IS TRUTH?)

What's true and what's not true in my grief, a question you might have asked yourself. You believed in Truth, but also asked, What is Truth?

The truth was this: you were dying.

A friend said, "David, Nikos is gone." I said, "But I want him." The friend said, "Yes, you want him, but he's gone, David, he's gone."

When our housekeeper, Maria, came, I met her on the stairs. We went together to the bedroom where now you, in a coma, were alone. Maria embraced me forcefully to her tiny body, tears dripping down her face. She let go of me and, turning to you, shouted, "*Che Gesù Cristo apra le sue braccia e prenda Nicola a Lui,*"[7] then she turned away from you and said, in disgust, "*Se cè un Gesù Cristo.*"[8] But she went to you, in your deep coma, and made the sign of the cross with her thumb on your forehead and kissed you on the forehead.

If only, I thought, you would simply disappear. If only you wouldn't leave your lifeless body behind. I would not be able to bear that, your body left behind after you died.

---

7. "That Jesus Christ open his arms and take Nicola to him."
8. "If there is a Jesus Christ."

I had a horror of dreaming about you after you died.

No one, no one else in all the world, was dying, no one but you.

I was in a daze of conflicting emotions, and one was that none of the others mattered.

If memory selects, why does it select for me to see you in a coma, your body covered with purple bedsores that shocked me as I helped the night nurse wash you? And why does memory center for all my life the moment you stopped breathing, when I, come into the room from the study where I'd been sleeping, saw you suddenly breathe out, and not breathe in?

The shock of seeing you breathe out and not breathe in made me stand back and exclaim, "He's dead," that shock displacing me to a periphery from where I saw this other self, no longer me, his hand across his mouth, speechless.

Your eyes were closed, closed so only a faint white showed, but I, I wanted to perform the final act of possession of you, to say "I closed his eyes," and I pressed my palm against your lids to close your eyes completely.

I lay beside you and felt your warmth give way to cold, so quickly.

# Iota

*The griever prays that grief will come and purify him, prays that after the overwhelming devastation of grief, whatever remains of him will be simple and clear. And suddenly, grief overwhelms the griever at the sight of an old woman in a crowd carrying a small valise.*

My love for you was not enough—you died.

It seems to me that all events converge in one, all in your death, which makes of our love one moment, and that lasting no more than the moment of your death, now gone.

How can I love you, you beyond my loving you?

You liked W.H. Auden's "Dichtung und Wahrheit," in which he wrote, "of the many (far too many) love poems written in the first person I have read, the most convincing were either the fa-la-la's of a good-natured sensuality which made no pretense at serious love, or howls of grief because the beloved had died and was no longer capable of love."

Your best suit, which I chose from your wardrobe, along with a shirt, and socks and shoes and underwear, as if to dress you for life, I put aside for your burial.

Organized through the Greek consulate for "the repatriation" of your body, undertakers came to take you away. I could not watch this, but stood by a window, looking down at the street at the mortuary van, the back doors open. I saw the two undertakers, carrying a red body bag, slide the bag into the back of the van and shut the doors, saw them take off their black jackets, heard them joke with each other as they got into the front of the van, and saw the van being driven off. I recalled the number of times I'd seen you in a taxi driven off for a trip you always hated going on, and that I hated your going on.

I had no idea where you were taken to, to some place too far for me to go there. When the director of the funeral parlor called me, my first thought was, he wanted to tell me about the bill. He did, but also said that you were dressed and laid out, and asked if I would like to see you. I exclaimed, "I didn't know I could!" and wondered why I'd felt I couldn't.

I immediately went out for a taxi. The address—Myddleton Road, N22—was, the driver said, a long way. Rain fell, and he drove up Park Road, Wellington Road, up Finchley to Hampstead, from where London, gray-white and vast, appeared over the green trees of the Heath, and down Spaniards Road, a narrow cutting through dense green, then through Hampstead Garden Suburb, the road lined with grand houses, and then deeper and deeper into the outer

London of row houses with small cemented front gardens and bat-
tered dustbins and front windows with lace curtains, and around
Bounds Green Station to a road of dilapidated shops, one with a
window display of icons and hanging icon lamps and small Greek
flags, in the Greek Cypriot neighborhood—Cypriot and, the driver
told me, Indian mixed—and a newly built funeral parlor, with a
stark façade and wide shop windows in which were shown rows of
urns for ashes. I pushed a button by the stark wooden door, then,
no one answering, I looked through a shop window to see a man
behind a glass partition talking on the telephone. He, noting me,
raised a hand to let me know he'd be with me in a minute.


In his glass-partitioned office, I paid the bill and followed him,
across the entrance hall, to a door he opened onto a little room,
where he left me. You were laid out in the middle of the room in
a narrow coffin, behind you a small altar draped in red velvet and
on it a baroque wooden crucifixion, on either side baroque stands
supporting pale, upward-shining lights.


The taxi driver was waiting outside to bring me back to our
home.


We went together to Athens in an airplane, you in your coffin in
the hold and I among the passengers, for your burial. Julia and our
friends Tory and Mark, whose loving family was our family, came
to support me.

Over the open doors to the chapel in the cemetery in which your funeral service was held is a mosaic, in the Byzantine style, of an angel at a tomb, the slab fallen away, announcing that Christ is no longer there.

When, at your funeral service in the small cemetery chapel, the priest presented the icon to me to kiss, my hand, of itself, rose up to make the sign of the cross, from my left shoulder to my right, more the sign of an ancient schism between our Christian churches, mine Roman, yours Greek, than of my faith.

And I threw a handful of earth on your coffin within the pit.

Julia, still and silent, held me as I howled as the gravediggers heaped sand into the pit.

Your family tomb is in the Second Cemetery—Το Δεύτερο Νεκροταφείο—where so many refugees from the Catastrophe are buried, a little, walled city of marble temples and crosses.

You wanted to be buried with your family, not with me. Did I take this as a rejection or the fulfillment of your vision of you forever with your grandmother, your father, your mother, and your two aunts? In the last poem that you wrote, which I found after you had died, you ended with a vision of all your closest family rising happily, hand in hand, from death to get on with the tasks of life—you there now among them, to rise with them.

I cannot be buried with you, as I am not Greek Orthodox. Do I regret that I will not be buried with you? I know this: that we would not be united in our deaths if buried together. Death unites no one with no one and loves no one.

Yet, in writing about your death, I want to write: Ω Θάνατε! Oh Death!

# KAPPA

*And grief longs to give the griever what grief can't give, more than*
*the life and love of the beloved, more, much more.*

Back in our home alone, I, as though in a trance that gave me no
choice, lay awake in our bed, on your side, the side where you slept
and where you died.

I lay in our bed, in which lovemaking tangled us in sheets and
bound us, and where, bound, we fell asleep, as if the bed were our
final resting place. And here you died, here where I lay wide awake,
and, restless, thought I must throw out this creaking bed, and, too,
the pillows and the blankets and the sheets.

Drunk, drunk on wine, so drunk that I was not sure how to get
from the bedroom to the bathroom to vomit, all the while I thought
of how my life was disoriented, not knowing, in the drunkenness of
my grief, where I was, where I was going.

To hold the body of another as I held you revolts me for all that
keeps the body alive: the stinking fat, the bile, the slime, the shit,
which somehow contrive in functions that conceal the truth, that
belie the truth: the beauty of the body is the body's biggest lie.

# Lambda

*Grief centers the griever's grief everywhere, making connections.*

A friend wrote after you had died, describing you as "the simplest and the most sophisticated of men."

Someone who hardly knew you, but knew you well enough to be impressed, said about you, "I felt he had been through fire, and, seared, was purified to an essential."

You were, as a friend said, an ascetic with the most acute sense of the aesthetic.

Your old friend from your Harvard days said about you, "He died fulfilled, as a publisher, as a poet—and he loved you."

Thomas Neurath, the owner of Thames & Hudson, where you had been a director for thirty years (so many books you commissioned were dedicated to you!), wanted to give you a memorial, a recital of Bach partitas in the Rotunda of the National Gallery. To play, he asked Richard Goode, who accepted. Among the first to arrive, I climbed the wide stairs of the gallery and, at the top, stopped to look back, to see all our London friends rising up, rising up, rising up, hundreds of them to embrace, more friends than either of us had thought we had, including Natasha Spender, the widow of Stephen.

This poem of yours was read at the memorial:
*IMPERATIVE PRESENT*

*Maybe from all these fragments*
*The present will emerge one day which is not imperative*
*But simply present,*
*Neither of avoidance or task—the rules that force it to exist—*
*But itself, clear and simple.*
*And maybe then, at another level now beyond me*
*Where continuity will, I hope, bring together these forced fragments,*
*The present will be fecund with the ideal fecundity of now.*
*Without the fear of misunderstanding,*
*Maybe these words will then communicate what is unique to their sounds as I utter them.*

After Richard Goode's recital, a reception, with wine and Greek hors d'oeuvres, was held in the grand Venetian Room, where I noted the panoramic Veronese of *The Family of Darius before Alexander,* in which the mother of Darius begs pardon for having mistaken Haesphaestion for Alexander, beautiful Alexander, gesturing with acceptance to the mother with one hand and to Haesphaestion with the other, as if to let her know that she was right to take his lover for him, his lover being him. In the background, many of the almost transparent onlookers wear Turkish turbans.

# Mı

*At a theatre, above the proscenium arch, Apollo rides his golden*
*chariot, and the griever sees his dead lover being transported by*
*Apollo in his chariot, to wherever Apollo is going.*

All feeling and all thought, all, are absent in your absence, so
why, why is such total absence of thought and feeling so potent a
presence—yours?

The closer I get to the final feeling, the final thought about you
dead, the very feeling, the very thought, turns against itself as not
the final feeling, not the final thought.

Let loose, I tell myself, let loose all that I feel, let loose all that I
feel into grief, and, oh, let that grief expand and expand and expand,
so beyond me that grief ceases to be mine.

Is my final image of you dead one of pure emptiness, if pure
emptiness can be an image?

Let this be the final image of you: the image of your face when
you died, which so shocked me, has become the image of you in

your youth, in your beauty, so I grieve for you died young, died beautiful—you, or someone young and beautiful, someone heroic in his belief in pure love.

Like a gold death mask, I place over your face the ideal of Greek beauty.

*Your* Great Idea, η Μεγάλι σου Ιδέα, is Greece's imperial legacy, Greece's splendor: the belief in freedom, truth, beauty, and in love.

Alleluia, my Love, Alleluia, Alleluia.

Αλληλούια, αγάπη μου, Αλληλούια, Αλληλούια!